The World of
Winslow Homer

TIME LIFE BOOKS ®

Other Publications:

THE EPIC OF FLIGHT

THE GOOD COOK

THE SEAFARERS

THE ENCYCLOPEDIA OF COLLECTIBLES

THE GREAT CITIES

WORLD WAR II

HOME REPAIR AND IMPROVEMENT

THE WORLD'S WILD PLACES

THE TIME-LIFE LIBRARY OF BOATING

HUMAN BEHAVIOR

THE ART OF SEWING

THE OLD WEST

THE EMERGENCE OF MAN

THE AMERICAN WILDERNESS

THE TIME-LIFE ENCYCLOPEDIA OF GARDENING

LIFE LIBRARY OF PHOTOGRAPHY

THIS FABULOUS CENTURY

FOODS OF THE WORLD

TIME-LIFE LIBRARY OF AMERICA

GREAT AGES OF MAN

LIFE SCIENCE LIBRARY

THE LIFE HISTORY OF THE UNITED STATES

TIME READING PROGRAM

LIFE NATURE LIBRARY

LIFE WORLD LIBRARY

FAMILY LIBRARY:

   HOW THINGS WORK IN YOUR HOME

   THE TIME-LIFE BOOK OF THE FAMILY CAR

   THE TIME-LIFE FAMILY LEGAL GUIDE

   THE TIME-LIFE BOOK OF FAMILY FINANCE

TIME-LIFE LIBRARY OF ART

The World of Winslow Homer

1836-1910

by James Thomas Flexner
and
the Editors of TIME-LIFE BOOKS

Time-Life Books, Alexandria, Virginia

Time-Life Books Inc.
is a wholly owned subsidiary of
TIME INCORPORATED

FOUNDER: Henry R. Luce 1898-1967

Editor-in-Chief: Henry Anatole Grunwald
President: J. Richard Munro
Chairman of the Board: Ralph P. Davidson
Executive Vice President: Clifford J. Grum
Editorial Director: Ralph Graves
Vice Chairman: Arthur Temple

TIME-LIFE BOOKS INC.
MANAGING EDITOR: Jerry Korn
Executive Editor: David Maness
Assistant Managing Editors: Dale M. Brown (planning),
George Constable, George G. Daniels (acting),
Martin Mann, John Paul Porter
Art Director: Tom Suzuki
Chief of Research: David L. Harrison
Director of Photography: Robert G. Mason
Assistant Art Director: Arnold C. Holeywell
Assistant Chief of Research: Carolyn L. Sackett
Assistant Director of Photography: Dolores A. Littles

CHAIRMAN: Joan D. Manley
President: John D. McSweeney
Executive Vice Presidents: Carl G. Jaeger,
John Steven Maxwell, David J. Walsh
Vice Presidents: George Artandi (comptroller);
Stephen L. Bair (legal counsel); Peter G. Barnes;
Nicholas Benton (public relations); John L. Canova;
Beatrice T. Dobie (personnel); Carol Flaumenhaft
(consumer affairs); Nicholas J. C. Ingleton (Asia);
James L. Mercer (Europe/South Pacific); Herbert Sorkin
(production); Paul R. Stewart (marketing)

TIME-LIFE LIBRARY OF ART
Editorial Staff for *The World of Winslow Homer:*
EDITOR: Percy Knauth
Text Editor: David S. Thomson
Picture Editor: Jane Scholl
Designer: Paul Jensen
Assistant Designer: Leonard Wolfe
Chief Researcher: Martha T. Goolrick
Researchers: Susan Rayfield, Susanna Seymour,
Patricia Smalley

EDITORIAL PRODUCTION
Production Editor: Douglas B. Graham
Operations Manager: Gennaro C. Esposito,
Gordon E. Buck (assistant)
Assistant Production Editor: Feliciano Madrid
Quality Control: Robert L. Young (director), James J. Cox
(assistant), Daniel J. McSweeney, Michael G. Wight
(associates)
Art Coordinator: Anne B. Landry
Copy Staff: Susan B. Galloway (chief),
Muriel Clarke, Celia Beattie
Picture Department: Patricia Maye

About the Author

James Thomas Flexner, who here plays the dual role of author and consultant, has published more than a dozen books dealing with the American past. His book *That Wilder Image,* which traces the rise of a Native School of American painting, won the Parkman Prize, awarded annually by the Society of American Historians for the book that best demonstrates history as a branch of literature. In 1973 he received a Pulitzer Prize for his four-volume biography of George Washington.

The Consulting Editor

H. W. Janson is Professor Emeritus of Fine Arts at New York University. Among his numerous books and publications are his definitive *History of Art,* which ranges from prehistory to the present day, and *The Story of Painting for Young People,* which he co-authored with his wife.

On the Slipcase

Octant in hand, a seaman determines the position of his storm-tossed ship in this detail from Homer's classic *Eight Bells,* 1886.

End Papers

Two of Homer's monochrome watercolors, painted in Canada during the summer of 1895, show men enjoying the artist's favorite sport—fishing. *Front: Fisherman, Lake St. John, Canada,* The Cooper Union Museum. *Back: Two Men in a Canoe,* Mr. and Mrs. Charles Shipman Payson.

CORRESPONDENTS: Elisabeth Kraemer (Bonn); Margot Hapgood, Dorothy Bacon, Lesley Coleman (London); Susan Jonas, Lucy T. Voulgaris (New York); Maria Vincenza Aloisi, Josephine du Brusle (Paris); Ann Natanson (Rome). Valuable assistance was also provided by: Karin B. Pearce (London); Carolyn T. Chubet, Miriam Hsia, Christina Lieberman (New York); Mimi Murphy (Rome).

For information about any Time-Life book, please write:
Reader Information
Time-Life Books
541 North Fairbanks Court
Chicago, Illinois 60611

Contents

I

A Native
Vigor

The second half of the 19th Century was one of the greatest periods for painting in the history of the Western world, and one of the great painters of the era was the Yankee Winslow Homer. His youthful renditions of smiling American life, the work of his middle years which shows man warring heroically with savage nature, and the unpeopled seascapes of his old age—all these constitute a major American contribution to the artistic treasures of the human race.

Homer was a contemporary of such great French Impressionists as Manet, Renoir and Degas, and he worked in a manner that bore some resemblance to theirs but was at the same time quite different. Indeed, his canvases have seemed so strange to people unfamiliar with the artistic and social traditions of the broad but isolated continent from which Homer sprang that they have often regarded him as an almost inexplicable phenomenon. To understand Winslow Homer's life and work, it is essential to follow him into his own American environment.

Born in Boston, Massachusetts, on February 24, 1836, to a family whose roots went back on both the mother's and the father's sides for many generations in New England, Homer was a Yankee to the bone. He was always taciturn, like so many of his neighbors; in manhood his passion for privacy made him averse to autobiography and outraged if asked personal questions by the press. This reticence has left posterity with few written accounts of his personal feelings, although there are some notes on conversations with him, jotted down by his friends. And his paintings speak for his emotions: in the true Yankee manner, the pictures are quiet on the surface but burn with interior passion.

The man who in his later years painted such marvelous pictures of the ocean stemmed from a family that had always been connected with the sea—though his forebears were less often sailors than merchants who stayed ashore and bought and sold what the sea captains brought home from distant ports. Homer's father was an importer of hardware, and both his grandfathers had engaged in similar trades.

Homer's parents had that itch for movement common to so many Americans. Winslow was born at 25 Friend Street, in a comfortably

7

middle-class section of Boston. He was soon carried to a house near Bowdoin Square. The next shift took him, when he was about six, to the nearby university town of Cambridge, where the family first lived on Main Street (now Massachusetts Avenue) and then on Garden Street, across from the Cambridge Common.

Wherever they settled, the family possessed a tight inner cohesion: Winslow's closest associates till his death were the blood relations he had lived with in his childhood. His father, Charles Savage Homer, was an egotistical, affectionate, overoptimistic businessman who was beloved by his family but sometimes seemed to others a crackbrained promoter and a blowhard. There were Winslow's two brothers, Charles Savage Jr., two years older than he, and Arthur Benson, five years younger. The only feminine element was supplied by Winslow's mother, Henrietta Maria, who introduced into the roaring male household the gentler claims of art. In the 19th Century, drawing in watercolor was a treasured "female accomplishment" taught in finishing school. The results were hung in parlors as a kind of flypaper to entrap young men into proposing to young ladies so brimming with artistic soul. But once successfully married, most women put their brushes away. Not so Winslow Homer's mother. She continued to take lessons and to execute charming, bright, accurate and decorative pictures of flowers.

Winslow's interest in art developed early. Certainly he leaned over his mother's drawing board, fascinated to see the colors shaped, with the movements of her hand, into images. Certainly she exposed him to painting and its theories as they were visible and understood in Cambridge and nearby Boston.

During Winslow's formative years, the Boston area was among the most artistically conservative of cultivated American regions. The local connoisseurs testified to the intellectual rather than visual foundations of their taste by establishing the city's public art gallery in the wing of their library, the Athenaeum. They had read about Old Masters, and it was Old Masters that they wished to collect.

The problems involved in amassing—at that late date, across a broad ocean, and for small sums—flocks of Titians, Raphaels and Correggios were ameliorated by the abysmal ignorance of the Bostonians as to what pictures by such famous artists really looked like. They happily accepted frauds. Add that in those days, when less emphasis was placed on an artist's personal touch than on what he expressed, it was common in Europe as well as in America to make little distinction between an original and a good copy. But even good copies rarely penetrated to Boston.

The result was that the walls of the Athenaeum Gallery were checkered with terrible daubs, each of which carried on its label a celebrated name. The novelist Nathaniel Hawthorne decided that he had advanced in taste when he came to realize that some of the paintings in the Athenaeum were more unpleasant than others. As for Homer, it was probably when he was dragged as a boy through the musty halls while the sun shone outside on brighter images that he developed his indifference to the Old Masters that remained with him throughout his career.

Although they were expert at making dollars out of the financial resources of the American world, the Massachusetts intellectual leaders adhered stubbornly to a conviction, outmoded in the rest of the nation, that America had no indigenous artistic resources. Like the Old Masters, modern art should be imported—or, if a man wielded a brush on American soil, he should wield it in ways developed abroad.

Paradoxically, this American esthetic dependence had originally been an offshoot of American political independence. The generation that fought the Revolution had felt self-reliant in all matters, and had, indeed, produced painters like the Pennsylvanian Benjamin West who infused American ideas into the bloodstream of European art. But with independence, connoisseurs not only in Boston but throughout the United States were haunted by the realization that their new nation was separated by 3,000 miles of ocean from the European centers of culture. Furthermore, those Americans who had inherited knowledge and prosperity feared that, by releasing the masses, the American Revolution had unchained a Caliban who would tear culture to ribbons with his unwashed claws. If the United States were not to become a laughingstock to the cultured people of the Old World, so it was reasoned, what today would be called a "crash program" would have to be undertaken to bring European culture and taste to the American masses.

A country bumpkin gets a going-over from a "click of town bucks" in a watercolor painted in 1796 by Washington Allston while he was a Harvard freshman. The picture is from a Hogarthian series, *The Buck's Progress*, in which Allston lightheartedly traced the bumpkin's downfall. Allston showed promise of becoming the best American painter of his generation, but failed to achieve greatness.

The most dramatic result of this taste for European culture took place only a few miles from the house where Homer grew up. There stood the studio which correct Bostonians considered the very temple of American art. Surely Homer never visited there, since the idol in the temple shied away from grubby little boys who might have live toads in their pockets. But young Winslow must have known the story of Washington Allston, which remained the favorite artistic saga of Boston, and that story could not have encouraged him to seek inspiration in Europe or in the historical past.

Allston had started out gaily. He was handsome and, as the son of a South Carolina rice planter, rich. Born in 1779, he had gone to the institution at Homer's doorstep, Harvard College, and then in 1801 had sailed for Europe to become an artist. His student years over, Allston had stayed abroad, painting in London, in Paris, in Rome. Word of great triumphs came back to America: friendship with famous men like the English poet Samuel Taylor Coleridge, enthusiastic reviews, high reputation and great sales in that capital of English culture, London. What was the delight of Massachusetts connoisseurs when, after 17 triumphant European years, Allston announced that he would return to the United States and settle in Boston.

Allston brought with him in 1818 a tremendous, almost completed canvas based on the Bible: it showed Daniel terrifying the evil King Belshazzar during a riotous feast by reading his doom from the handwriting on the wall. This became known at once as "The Great Picture" and 10 of the country's most distinguished art patrons subscribed $1,000 apiece to buy it. Allston expected to finish *Belshazzar's Feast* in a few months. When Winslow Homer was born 18 years later, the picture was still uncompleted, although year after year the artist had painted on little else. He had become so sensitive on the matter that he would allow

In middle age, Samuel F. B. Morse was dismayed to find he could no longer sell flamboyant works such as his *Dying Hercules* *(above)*. He focused his energies instead on science and developed the telegraph. But, in a strange marriage of art and science, he used a wooden stretcher, such as he had employed to keep his canvases taut, as a frame for his first receiver. Nailing the stretcher to an ordinary table, he attached various instruments to it, including a pencil device (g) which recorded messages.

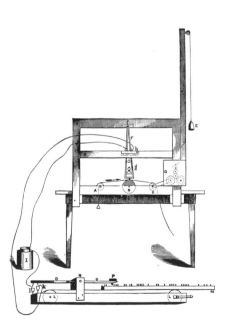

no one to ask about the unfinished work or to enter his studio, behavior which made the progress of the vast, mysterious masterpiece a favorite subject for speculation in the press. Allston died when Homer was seven and a reverential delegation of his friends pulled back the curtain that hid The Great Picture. What they saw was a monstrous, incoherent wreck.

Boston drew from this tale two morals, both of which Homer must have encountered again and again in publications on American art. One was that the United States was by its very nature esthetically barren. The Massachusetts-born sculptor William Wentworth Story, who had expatriated himself to Italy, wrote: "Allston starved spiritually in Cambridgeport. . . . There was nothing congenial without, and he turned all his powers inward and drained his memory dry." Homer's behavior as a painter—he was to avoid European study and paint the American scene —implies that he drew an opposite moral: If Allston had not felt superior to his American environment but had sought to draw strength from it, his art might not have withered.

Literary Boston's second explanation of Allston's failure was that the painter's thoughts had been so noble that they had transcended the possibilities of paint. Thus, in the words of a local historian, Allston's very frustration proved him "an artist in the highest and fullest sense of the word . . . the only old master of modern times." Perhaps the annoyance of the practical-minded young Homer at such highfalutin talk helped incline him never to theorize on art, but to stick to his easel.

Allston's two major coadjutors in trying to import European styles into the United States were John Vanderlyn and Samuel F. B. Morse. Born in New York State, Vanderlyn made himself over in Paris, where he won the gold medal of the Salon for his huge reconstruction of Roman times, *Marius Amid the Ruins of Carthage (page 19)*. He returned to the United States after 19 expatriate years determined to elevate what he considered the debased taste of America by continuing to paint scenes from classical times. However, like Allston, he found that inspiration flagged. As Homer grew to eager young manhood, Vanderlyn grew into a sterile old man pontificating angrily that no one but "a professional quack" could paint in America.

Morse, the son of a leading Connecticut minister and geographer, started his artistic career, after his graduation from Yale, in London as a pupil of Allston's. "My ambition," he wrote, "is to be among those who shall revive the splendor of the fifteenth century; to rival the genius of a Raphael, a Michel Angelo, or a Titian." Toward this end, he painted a larger-than-life-sized picture called *Dying Hercules*. His money having run out, he was forced to come home. In America, he found a brisk demand for portraiture, which he supplied with excellent paintings. However, his training would not let him take seriously this unexalted branch of art. He was delighted when in 1837, the year after Homer's birth, he was at last commissioned to create one of those ambitious historical compositions on which he hoped his reputation would be based. But his pleasure soon changed to chagrin. He found that, like Allston and Vanderlyn, he had lost his inspiration. In mounting despair, he stood before a huge oblong of canvas day after day. Finally, he threw down his brushes, concentrated his attention on the problems of his environment and invented the telegraph.

Rarely have environment and the movement of history taken such summary revenge on a group of artists who willfully attempted to ignore them. Allston, Vanderlyn and Morse had tried to pull up their American roots without putting down any effective roots elsewhere. They had attempted to superimpose on the United States an art which, whatever its validity (or lack of validity) in other countries, surely had little reference to the active realities and attitudes of their own blossoming land.

I t can be argued that the art which the Americans were trying to import had among its philosophical bases disillusionment with contemporary life. In the late 18th Century, Europe had been buoyed up by a belief in the perfectibility of man which the success of the American Revolution had done much to encourage. The French Revolution had at first seemed another step in the liberation of the human spirit. But high hope and idealism had given way to the pound of the guillotine; savagery had taken over in France. The Napoleonic Wars had again raised democratic hopes throughout Europe only to trample them into blood-soaked mud. Following the defeat of Napoleon, there came into power almost everywhere despotisms that were afraid to let the minds or emotions of men run free. Damaged hope urged artists all over Europe to turn their backs on everything contemporary. The "noble," the "spiritual," the "sublime," which had often seemed to earlier romantic artists to reside in the actual world, were now sought almost exclusively in the past, in the exotic, in the imaginary. Following this trend, Allston and Vanderlyn and Morse had painted Belshazzar and Marius and Hercules, none of whom, needless to say, had much relevance to American life.

In the early 19th Century the United States, unlike Europe, was moving toward more freedom and wider democracy. The War of 1812 marked America's last major involvement before 1914 in European conflicts. The Monroe Doctrine of 1823 ordered Europe out of the Western Hemisphere. Looking no more across the ocean, the United States turned toward its own undeveloped lands, becoming absorbed in the riches there. The frontiersman Andrew Jackson marched from Tennessee to the Presidency, and his inauguration horrified American gentility by allowing rough Western manners to pass through the classic portals of the White House. The connoisseurs dug in their heels, all the more determined to keep American art tied to European taste, but it was as much a losing battle as King Canute's when he told the waves to stand still.

The physical symbol of the new age was the Erie Canal which, by channeling water from the Great Lakes down to the Hudson River, opened cheap communication between America's great central valley and New York City. One result was that Homer's Boston, which had no good means of communication with the West, became a relative backwater: New York was now the leading metropolis of the United States. It was surely no coincidence that in the metropolis, during the very year of the opening of the Erie Canal, 1825, the artistic tables turned.

In extreme silence, the smallest sound is heard. As American painting, its leading practitioners all sterile, lay motionless in cultural winter, behind the window of a New York frame shop there appeared three canvases by a stripling named Thomas Cole. He was utterly unknown to the connoisseurs and his pictures were a rapturous denial of all imported canons of taste. They were not learned; they did not deal with the past; their subject matter had no reference to anything European. They were direct and eloquent renditions of scenery on the Hudson River some miles upstream from New York. Yet passersby were stopped in their tracks; Cole was summoned from his lodgings to meet leaders of American taste; and there, as voices rose in excitement, a Native School of American painting was born. The greatest figure in that school was to be Winslow Homer.

Americans had been so blind to the beauties of their own land that it had taken an immigrant to point that loveliness out to them: Cole had been born in England, where artists had for some time been concerned with their own local scenery. When Cole followed their lead in America, native Americans were overwhelmed. The poet William Cullen Bryant remembered being "delighted at the opportunity of contemplating pictures which carried the eye to a scene of wild grandeur peculiar to our country, over our aerial mountain tops, with their mighty growth of forest never touched by the axe, along the banks of streams never deformed by culture, and into the depths of skies bright with the hues of our own climate, such as few but Cole could paint. . . ."

Raised in England's Lancashire County, the very cradle of the Industrial Revolution, Cole, at the age of 18, had escaped from the palls of smoke that hid his natal skies by leading his parents on a romantic flight to America. He later wrote, "I would give my left hand to identify myself with this country by being able to say I was born here." Once over the mountains in the Ohio Valley, Cole made himself a professional artist in a manner as old as settlement in America. He went to no art school. He did few student exercises. Having resolved to set up as a portrait painter, he bought materials, induced people to pose, and, after a week or two of experimentation, earned his living from the results. With his painting materials on his back, he walked the roads and knocked on doors, a peddler of portraits.

Cole soon discovered that he was less interested in human faces than in the face of Nature: he applied his portrait approach to landscape. When he finally got to an art school, The Pennsylvania Academy of the Fine Arts, he ignored the objections raised by his teachers against painting American views.

In the 19th Century, as this wood engraving from *Harper's Weekly* humorously shows, itinerant portraitists were often paid for their work in kind rather than money. Thomas Cole received a saddle for the first portrait he painted. As his biographer noted: "While no one . . . was so liberal as to bring him a horse . . . there came an ugly-looking militia officer, and a dapper tradesman, whose united pay for their portraits was an old silver watch, and a chain and key that turned out to be copper."

Guided only by his own untutored eyes, Cole had started at the most advanced point reached by landscape painting up to that time: naturalistic renditions of Nature for her own sake. He continued to paint in this manner, but as increasing sophistication descended upon him, he also tried some of the modes of painting being practiced in Europe. The poet Alexander Pope had spoken for the 18th Century when he wrote that "the proper study of mankind is man." This philosophy, which held among other things that wild nature, being uncouth, was an unworthy subject for art, persisted into the 19th Century and prompted artists to modify pure landscapes with human sentiment expressed in various forms. Cole occasionally succumbed to these older ideas, creating nostalgic views of culture-haunted Italy which showed the crumbling remains of vanished human glories. He also reconstructed medieval times. He even painted moral allegories, garnished with angels. These paintings were hailed by the old guard of American connoisseurs, but the people took to their hearts Cole's unheightened views of American scenery, the pictures which started the Native School on its triumphant way.

As far advanced as Cole's Native School pictures were, he was not, of course, the initiator of the naturalistic landscape approach. That honor belonged to the Englishman John Constable, who was 25 years Cole's senior and was already widely recognized as one of the world's greatest landscapists. However, when Cole visited London as the established leader of the American landscape school, he did not exclude Constable when he wrote, "I cannot but think that I have done more than any of the English painters." Their work, he continued, "disgusted with its gaud and ostentation. . . . The standard," Cole explained, "by which I form my judgement is beautiful nature."

The fact is that each man was being true to his subject. Cole's conception of "beautiful nature" had been burned into his brain by the American landscape, while Constable had developed his style to render English scenery, which actually is more brightly colored. "Nothing," Cole himself had written, "can be a richer green than an English lawn." America had tannish meadows rather than lawns and, almost everywhere, trees in various shades of dark green. The onetime mayor of New York, Philip Hone, wrote that Cole's "landscapes are too solid, massy, and umbrageous to please the eye of an amateur accustomed to Italian skies and English-park scenery, but I think every American is bound to prove the love of his country by admiring Cole."

The group of landscape painters which Cole led into being were to be described as the Hudson River School. The name came naturally, since the artists individually and cooperatively worked out their techniques primarily to paint the beautiful region where the Catskill Mountains met in variegated wildness the cultivated shores of the Hudson River. Emphasizing individual and native inspiration, the Hudson River artists believed that only after a young painter had formed his own impressions from personal examination of American nature could he accept instruction or study any other man's pictures to his advantage.

The American land spoke somewhat differently to different artists, yet certain imperatives were accepted by Cole and by all his direct followers. It was a huge land, and realization of its size kept the painters from typically depicting restricted glades. They preferred the shaggy hills to the pastoral meadows and the wild to the tame. The American land pitched every which way; fields were holes in foliage and paths were gullies, ruts lined the roads, stones shouldered upward between furrows, and almost every vista featured the irregular, spiky shapes of treetops.

Fascinated with specific phenomena, the Hudson River artists wished to generalize as little as possible, and yet they had so much to paint, such huge vistas to show! This dilemma forced Cole and his followers into technical expedients more common in medieval work than in the sophisticated arts of modern Europe. Instead of painting a view as it would appear from a single vantage point, the Hudson River artists came close to paint some details and then moved back to encompass the whole prospect—which means that the viewer cannot appreciate the picture from one position in a gallery but also has to step back and forth. Some critics consider this simply an artistic failure, but it served well to express the complexity of the American scene.

The traditional landscapists of Europe often placed in their foregrounds men staring into the view, to make it clear that they were showing nature as refigured in the mind of man. In his naturalistic landscapes, Cole gave humanity no such star billing. Men were on an equality with plants and animals, being among the details the viewer must come near to the canvas to see: a field, for example, will prove on close scrutiny to have in it a boy chasing horses.

All those aspects of Cole's work that he had borrowed from Europe —nostalgic views of ruins, historic reconstructions, storytelling landscapes—faded with his death from the main line of American painting. His most influential follower, Asher B. Durand, considered such pictures "studied artificiality and imbecile attempts" suited to "the tourist and the historian" rather than the true landscapist. A landscape, Durand wrote, was "great in proportion as it declares the glory of God, not the works of man."

Durand was born in New Jersey in 1796 to a family of high-spirited artisans who made inventions for fun and farmed for their livelihood. Unlike Cole but like all his fellow Hudson River School artists, Durand was a birthright member of the American Elysium. He did not share with Cole any interior pull between Old World teachings and American experience. He had always inhabited an abundant continent that showered prosperity on the self-reliant. While half of Cole's mind wondered whether Nature did not contain much evil, Durand and his colleagues believed wholeheartedly that the world was good and that a beneficent Deity manifested Himself in things as they were.

In 1855 and 1856, when Winslow Homer was turning 20, Durand brought out a series of "Letters on Landscape Painting" which define better than any other publication the basic tenets of the Hudson River School. Nature in its purity, Durand stated, "is fraught with high and holy meaning, only surpassed by the light of Revelation." A painting that evoked "the same feelings and emotions which we experience in the presence of reality" was a visual sermon, an active force urging man to a nobler life. This conception overcame the fear—which had long haunted some Americans—that art might be a trap baited by aristocracies and the Roman Catholic Church to enmesh Protestant democrats in enervating luxuries and Romish doctrines. Pragmatic Protestant minds were drawn to pictures that disseminated God's handiwork. Such pictures hung naturally on the wall over the family Bible.

Even as it would be blasphemy to rewrite the Bible, the Hudson River

Wandering through the countryside looking for views to paint, Thomas Cole made careful sketches, often of anthropomorphic trees like this strange trunk. He evolved a whole philosophy of trees, seeing "an expression of affection in intertwining branches,—of despondency in the drooping willow." But in the presence of those growing on mountaintops he seemed almost frightened. They "grasp the crags with their gnarled roots," he wrote, "and struggle with the elements with wild contortions."

painters, Durand wrote, should not tamper with those natural beauties that were "types of divine attributes." Yet the painters did not seek what Durand called "servile imitation." The artist was not an ordinary man. Walking through nature, he saw more than the less sensitive, less dedicated layman at his side. And he created his picture to bring within the grasp of the layman the painter's greater perceptions. The artist, indeed, played very much the same role as the preachers in the evangelical religions which swept mid-19th Century America. God, according to their theology, lived in every man's heart, but a sinner's mind and emotions needed to be sensitized into recognition of the Divine Word. The Austrian scholar Fritz Novotny argues that the great struggle of 19th Century European art was to achieve a synthesis between the real and the ideal. The Native School did not suffer from this dichotomy. Living in a happy world, Americans insisted that the ideal was not opposed to the real but was instead its perfection.

Out of the artists' religious base grew the characteristic that most separates the Hudson River School—and, indeed, the Native School as a whole—from much of European art. Even as a preacher who heard God speaking in his own breast would not distort the expression of this Inner Light by his own idiosyncrasies and temperament, so the painters wished to give, as far as possible, the impression that their pictures were not objects made by individual men but actual slices of Nature. Homer was to agree wholeheartedly with the Hudson River School doctrine that skill should be used not to impress the viewer with an artist's virtuosity or temperament, but so to subordinate means to ends that the means disappear and only the ends are perceived. A landscape should not be a demonstration of the painter's technique. Rather, it should make the viewer feel as if he were actually in the presence of Nature at its most sublime. Even the mood of the picture should be revealed as not the artist's but the landscape's own.

The connoisseurs and the painters whose imitative styles the Native School had superseded had complained that the American public was too clodlike to support art. The people had not, it is true, enjoyed what was being forced down their throats as cultural medicine. However, when an art appeared that expressed their own ideas about their own world, they clamored to buy and hang the pictures. Although Homer's Boston was outside the mainstream, the United States into which Winslow Homer was born was the proud possessor of a school of painters who insisted on their native inspiration and were wildly popular with most of their compatriots.

As one of the world's great painters, Homer was to carry the Native School approach far beyond any conceptions ever dreamed of by its early practitioners. However, that approach remained always the foundation on which he built his artistic achievements. He was, indeed, to adhere doggedly to Native School attitudes through a second period in which some American artists surrendered to fashions that failed to engage their deepest sympathies and emotions. If this steadfastness temporarily obscured Homer's reputation, it proved in the end to be a major source of his strength.

Nature's Dome

While Winslow Homer was growing up, the foundations of his own great art were being laid down by the Hudson River School. Sharing a passionate regard for nature, its convivial members had taken to themselves the wild, dramatic vistas of the Hudson River valley and the Catskill Mountains. "The painter of American scenery," commented Thomas Cole, founder of the movement, "has, indeed, privileges superior to any other. All nature here is new to art."

Responding to this newness, to this "something not found elsewhere," the pioneering artists of the Hudson River School—most of whom were self-taught—produced poetic and romantic landscapes like the atmospheric valley shown opposite. And for 50 years, throughout much of Homer's lifetime, they flourished. Although Homer cannot properly be counted among them, he too found his inspiration in America, and he carried into the 20th Century their best qualities—independence, honesty, naturalism.

Today, the members of the Hudson River School are being rediscovered and re-appraised, and their work once again admired. Their paintings do more than show the America that was. They tell how Americans felt about their pristine land at a time when it did not seem at all strange for a landscape painter like Thomas Cole to urge his fellow countrymen to come and kneel with him in "nature's everlasting dome."

Kindred Spirits is Asher B. Durand's memorial to Thomas Cole, key figure in the Hudson River School. It shows Cole admiring the beauties of the Catskills with his friend, the poet William Cullen Bryant. Durand believed that in painting scenes like this, American landscapists would evolve "a high and independent style."

Asher B. Durand: *Kindred Spirits*, 1849

17

Washington Allston: *Elijah in the Desert*, 1818

Samuel F. B. Morse: *Allegorical Landscape Showing New York University*, 1836

John Vanderlyn: *Marius Amid the Ruins of Carthage*, 1807

Before the advent of the Hudson River School, nature on its own terms was not considered an appropriate subject for the serious American painter. Washington Allston devised a purely imaginary landscape for his *Elijah in the Desert (top, left)*, a work that he had done in England from powdered colors mixed with skim milk and had glazed for an Old Master effect. Samuel F. B. Morse took nature apart and put it back together again in his *Allegorical Landscape (bottom, left)*, producing a painting so self-consciously sublime that it is hard to believe that the Gothic structure by the lagoon actually existed. But exist it did: it was the old New York University building on Washington Square, and in years to come one of its towers would serve Winslow Homer as a studio. John Vanderlyn made nature over into a stage prop, the background for his austere Marius *(above)* who sits, more statue than human being, on the ruins of Carthage. It remained for the untrained, English-born painter Thomas Cole to discover in the American landscape a great potential for art.

19

Cole: *Past*, 1838

Cole: *Present*, 1838

From his early youth onward, Thomas Cole was a walker. As an itinerant portraitist in the 1820s, he walked through Ohio in search of commissions. When this career failed him, he walked from Pittsburgh to Philadelphia wrapped in his mother's tablecloth—he was too poor to afford an overcoat. Even when success caught up with him, he walked, finding in his wanderings through the Catskill Mountains the stuff of his paintings and his dreams. "How I have walked," he exclaimed, "day after day, and all alone, to see if there was not something among the old things which

was new!" Confronted by the wilderness, he would often burst into song, or rush to set his impressions down in poetry. Walking "with nature as a poet" was prerequisite, he felt, to becoming a perfect artist.

Cole considered his finest work to be his allegorical paintings. Among the several he did in this vein are *Past* and *Present*, reproduced at left above. *Past* is his romanticized view of the Middle Ages; *Present* shows the same scene gone hopelessly to ruin. But despite his objections to being known as a "mere leaf painter," Cole is thought of today as having been at his

Thomas Cole: *View on the Catskill, Early Autumn*, 1837

best in his interpretations of Catskill scenery, as in the sylvan scene above. Here are the characteristics that his biographer called "all American" —"bright, polished waters, manifold woods . . . sweet glad light and quiet air." The wilderness still holds sway, but spotted throughout the painting are signs of man's encroachment on nature's domain—a farmhouse in the middle distance, a man in a boat, a boy chasing horses in a field, a hunter returning home after a day in the woods. The woman in the foreground presenting a child with a bouquet may be Cole's wife, to

whom the artist had been married only a short while.

All that Cole portrayed here so reverently was destined to change, and soon. "I took a walk, last evening, up the Valley of the Catskill, where they are now constructing the railroad," he noted in his journal. "This was once my favourite walk; but now the charm of solitude and quietness is gone." Without realizing it, he had not only written nature's obituary but he had also defined the quality that sets apart many another Hudson River School painting —the charm of solitude and quietness.

21

W̲hat was it in the American landscape that attracted the Hudson River School painters? Of what did that "something not found elsewhere" consist? There was the virgin wilderness, with the all-pervasive green of the undisturbed forests darker than that of Europe's parks and copses. But more importantly, and more subtly, there was the light—pure, and made infinitely variable by the abruptly changing seasons. How really different the light was in America became apparent to John F. Kensett and Worthington Whittredge upon their return from lengthy periods of European study. Whittredge managed to capture its clear radiance in his *Window, House on the Hudson (right)*. Here all outdoors seems to stream in through the open casement, flooding the room with a rich, warm light. A similar radiance pervades Kensett's coast scene *(below)*. As a friend of his put it, eulogizing the man who had become one of 19th Century America's most beloved artists: "He made sunshine that softened and harmonized all."

John F. Kensett: *Cliffs at Newport, R.I., Low Tide*, 1867

22

Worthington Whittredge: *Window, House on the Hudson*, 1863

Church: *Parthenon*, 1871

Church: *Niagara*, 1857

Church: *Iceberg*, 1891

Frederic Church was another Hudson River School painter obsessed with light—but light at its most grandiloquent. What Cinemascope is to the present age, Church, it might be said, was to his: the master of the spectacular view. His heroic canvases amounted, in the multiplicity and accuracy of their details, to visual encyclopedias of nature. It was as important to pore over them inch by inch as it was to see them whole; one of his exhibitors actually urged viewers to bring opera glasses with them so that they could explore the mighty landscape on display.

But where most of his fellow artists were content to paint American scenery, and Eastern scenery at that, Church roamed far afield. Out of one of his journeys came *Cotopaxi (left)*, an apocalyptic vision of an Ecuadorean volcano in which the rising sun has turned a lake into a crucible of molten copper.

The public thronged to see Church's work. His *Niagara (top, middle)* soon became one of America's best-known landscape paintings. To one admirer all it lacked was the roar of rushing water. When it was sold at auction in 1876 after being exhibited abroad it brought $12,500, a fortune in those days.

Church outlasted his own popularity: by the 1880s his paintings were out of style. He lived on, a rich but disillusioned man, in his mansion overlooking the Hudson—an architectural fantasy that he described as Persian and called Olana, "our place on high." The victim of a progressively crippling disease, Church was unable to paint at all during the last five years of his life. When he died in 1900, few remembered that he had once been called "the Michelangelo of landscape art."

Frederic Edwin Church: *Cotopaxi*, 1862

25

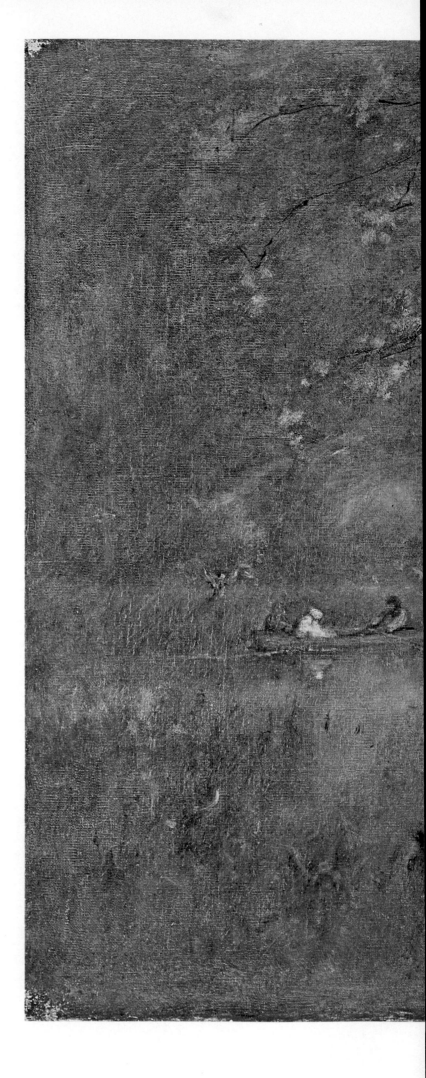

With the works of George Inness, American
landscape painting took a new turn. While
preserving the independence and poetry of men like
Cole and Durand, in whose footsteps he had at first
followed, Inness abandoned objective naturalism in
pursuit of what he called the "subjective mystery
of nature." *Pool in the Woods*, painted toward
the end of his career, shows how much he changed
the landscape form. Gone is the old Hudson River
School insistence upon the wide view and minute
detail, and in its place is a softening of trees
and foliage, a quiet music that rises from a synthesis
of color, brushwork and composition. There is a
mystical aura to his mature work. Inness had
fallen under the influence of Emanuel Swedenborg,
an 18th Century visionary, whose descriptions
of the spiritual world resemble the artist's
interpretations of nature.

Unlike his contemporary, Church, Inness
achieved success quite late in life. All through
the years he had hung on, evolving his own style,
managing somehow to support a wife and six
children, and combating as best he could the
epilepsy that afflicted him. More often than his
Hudson River School predecessors, Inness traveled
to Europe, where he admired a wide variety of
landscape styles, old and new. Learning from all, he
succumbed to none. He went his own way, painting
with zeal, sometimes spending 12 to 15 hours at a
stretch in front of his easel and repainting a canvas
six or more times. Modest and unpretentious, he
saw the artist's aim as "simply to reproduce in other
minds the impression which a scene had made upon
him." In his individualism he was like that other
Yankee painter—Winslow Homer.

George Inness: *Pool in the Woods*, 1892

II

Apprenticeship in Black and White

When the Homers moved from Boston to nearby Cambridge, six-year-old Winslow escaped from the streets of what was then America's fifth largest city to a village where great trees shimmered overhead like coherent flocks of green birds. Although within sight of Harvard College, the child was also within easy rambling distance of the very different art academy patronized by the Native School: the American countryside. Homer as a middle-aged man was to attribute his "great liking for country life"—so an interviewer wrote—to "the meadows, ponds, fishing, and beautiful surroundings of that suburban place." Perhaps it would not have struck him so hard had he been born in Cambridge—but to meet it all at the ecstatic age of six!

Homer was sent to a local grammar school. Never flamboyant in his behavior, always correct in any situation from which there was no escape, he seemed to one of his classmates "studious, quiet, sedate." However, he was not by nature addicted to sitting indoors. His attitude toward lessons is summarized in a marvelous painting called *Country School* which he executed years later, when he was 35. In this picture *(page 41)* it is clearly a hot day in late spring. Sunlight floods the schoolroom and the viewer can almost hear the sleepy droning of flies. The teacher is pretty but abstracted, her mind on something more basic to her nature than the book she holds in her hand. Some of the children are in ragged clothes although, being offspring of the American peasantry, they are all healthy and well fed. Their faces bear no anger or discontent: only a tedium that matches their teacher's. Outside, through the window, Homer painted the true joy and meaning of life: Nature in her wonder.

When Winslow was 13, his father gave way to a strong romantic streak: he sold his hardware business, invested the money in mining machinery and was off to the West Coast to take part in the Gold Rush of 1849. This adventure was a complete and costly failure. The resulting dip in the family fortunes protected Homer from what he had undoubtedly dreaded—sitting in Harvard classrooms after graduation from high school—but menaced him with an even worse fate: standing

Father Homer's trip to join the
Gold Rush prompted 13-year-old Winslow
to depict the event in a cartoon. Astride a
rocket that looks suspiciously like a fishing fly,
the father manages to cross the Rockies
before crashing on a group of forty-niners.

behind the counter of a nearby clothing store that needed a clerk.

At the moment of imminent danger, when Winslow was 19, his good fairy appeared, probably at the family breakfast table and certainly disguised as a newspaper advertisement. The father read it out: "Boy wanted; apply to Bufford, lithographer; must have taste for drawing; no other wanted."

That the lad had a taste for drawing was notorious. His mother had encouraged him from the start and his father, when on a visit to London, had sent him lithographs by French drawing teachers of heads, ears, noses, faces, trees, houses and animals that a student might copy. Of these models, Homer remembered, he made "profitable" use under parental eyes. Another artistic activity he pursued "stealthily" though "systematically": he brought life into his schoolbooks by illuminating the blank pages and margins. He found it most fun, however, to use his art to preserve glorious moments of play in the outdoors. Unlike the drawings of most children, his were not fantastic or exaggerated. His objective was already that of the Native School: to record happy images as they actually presented themselves to the eye. One early sketch shows a boy lying on his stomach dreaming away a summer's afternoon. Homer's earliest known watercolor, done at 11, is an excellent representation of a snug farmhouse surrounded by shade trees *(page 41)*.

Homer's art was still altogether private, an aspect of play which he did not wish the responsibilities of adulthood to interrupt. He was doubtless far from delighted when his father suggested that it would be easy to get him the job at Bufford's print-making establishment since Bufford and the elder Homer belonged to the same volunteer fire company. However, in due course a paper was signed. Winslow was to serve as an apprentice until he was 21, a period of two years which were to seem so endless that he was to remember them as three. The father would pay $300 for the first year's instruction; after that, the lad would receive five dollars a week. All this would be binding if, after two weeks' trial, Winslow was found to suit.

Winslow suited so well that the $300 fee was reduced to $100, but he remained resentful. Homer possessed an extremely youthful spirit —it was a quality which would enable him to react, deep into middle age, with the freshness of an adolescent—and, although he was 19, he felt he was much too young to be made to work. More than 40 years later the grievance was still there. An interviewer recalled that "he remarked with some pathos in his voice that while other boys were enjoying boyish play, he had his nose to the grindstone from eight in the morning till six in the evening, and that about his only recreation was an occasional hour's fishing in the early morning on his way to the shop. He said he would get up early, fish an hour, and then push his rod under some bushes to await another time."

The lithographer's shop closed around Homer even more tightly than schoolrooms had. His task was to draw on a specially prepared stone with a greasy crayon which attracted the ink that was to be transferred to the printed sheet. He worked standing, telling his fellow apprentices that if he sat down he might become round-shouldered. They remembered him as short and slight, very straight and energetic. His early morning bouts of fishing never showed in his costume, which was always so dapper that one of his companions suspected he possessed some hidden source of wealth.

A drawing made at the time by a friend *(page 43)* shows that he wore his dark brown hair long, a thick lock standing upright over his forehead, wings going off to both sides. His wide, downturned eyebrows were echoed in reverse by a moustache that rose at the tips. From his chin sprouted a goatee that looks svelte in the drawing but that in fact bothered him by coming out in patches. One suspects that he spent much time at the mirror deciding how he looked best.

Behind this correct and somewhat elfin appearance, Homer hid his emotions. In the shop he was quiet: when praised he said nothing; when criticized he showed no annoyance, efficiently making the changes suggested. But he hated the work, so much so that, although there were inherent in the lithographic medium great artistic possibilities, he never afterward put it to any effective use.

The difficulty seems to have been that Nature was excluded from Bufford's. The shop manufactured illustrations. There was no time or need, and even less desire, for anything freshly thought out or directly observed. Homer was expected to provide what had proved salable by adapting pictures taken from the company files.

He started by doing the title pages for sheet music—"Katy Darling" and "Oh Whistle and I'll Come to You, My Lad" were two of them—pictures as tedious to the eye as they obviously were to his hand. He worked up to making a large print of the Massachusetts Senate: 42 heads, mostly copied from photographs.

But Homer's ambition to become an artist was not stifled. Visiting a Boston art gallery with several fellow apprentices, he told them: "I am going to paint." When asked how he intended to work, he pointed to a kitchen scene by the then celebrated Frenchman, Edouard Frère: "Something like that, only a damned sight better." In the true Native School manner, he announced, "If a man wants to be an artist, he should never look at pictures."

Homer had decided that when he escaped from Bufford he would never take another job, but he did not feel ready to start painting. He resolved instead to become a free-lance draftsman. He would teach himself a new method of illustration then sweeping into America, the woodblock engraving. This decision carried him along a familiar Native School path, but with a significant difference.

During the Colonial period, the population of America had been so thinly scattered over so wide an area that no goods—not cloth nor tools nor pictures—could be economically produced for wide distribution. However, at about the same time that the Native School exploded into prominence, the population of the Eastern Seaboard had reached a density that could support shops producing printed pictures. Engravers also found employment making paper currency for the state and local banks that in the era of President Jackson issued much of the nation's folding money. The bills had to be elaborately printed and illustrated to frustrate counterfeiters. As the economy expanded, there was an ever-increasing demand for currency, and supplying the need was highly profitable for engravers. Thus, the flourishing industry beckoned to young men interested in art. Most of the Native School artists worked, until they could support themselves with their paintings, in such engraving establishments. Asher B. Durand had led the procession, having produced a variety of engravings, including bank notes, before he had become the leader of the Hudson River School.

In those days the finest work done by engravers was cutting small plates that would, although printed in black and white, convey the effect of large, multicolored oil paintings. The most elaborate of such prints were sold individually. Publishers who wished to sell some of these costly plates to a large market brought them out in periodicals which appeared once a year. Given such titles as *The Token* or *Friendship's Offering*, these pocket-sized, leather-bound volumes occupied the same position in the book market as do the huge, coffee-table volumes of color reproductions now offered as gifts for the Christmas season.

Lower costs and better distribution gradually made illustrated monthlies economically worthwhile but, as both population and prosperity skyrocketed, the demand for picture magazines far outran existing technology. The standard engraved plate, in addition to being expensive to make and also to print, took so much time to cut that it could not be used to depict anything very up-to-date. Lithography, the art Homer had learned at Bufford's, did not permit large pressruns: the plates rapidly grew dim with use.

An example of the kind of work Asher B. Durand did before becoming a leading landscape painter is the vignette above, designed and engraved by him for use on the five-dollar bank note below. It was hoped that engravings like this one—in which a partially clad woman quenches the thirst of an eagle—would help make paper currency "an instrument for refining public taste."

The problem, like the rise of the masses, was international. It was solved first in Europe through new applications of an old woodcut technique. First a block of boxwood would be prepared with a smooth surface. Then an artist would draw a picture—often directly on the wood—that would reproduce effectively in the medium. Finally a craftsman would carve the block, cutting away the wood surface in the spaces between the drawn lines, thereby leaving the design in relief. The result when inked would print beside type and in the same manner. When a large number of prints were required, the relatively soft woodblock was not actually used to do the printing, its design instead being transferred through a simple mechanical process to a metal plate. If a large picture of a news event were needed quickly, the boxwood could be sawed into several parts and, after each part had been cut by a different workman, the whole clamped together again so cleverly that the breaks hardly showed on the printed page.

This relatively swift woodblock technique made it possible to publish weekly newspapers heavily illustrated with cheaply produced topical pictures. However, before the demand for such publications could be supplied in the United States, workmen had to be procured who were skillful in each half of the process: artists who understood the medium and skilled cutters to prepare the blocks for the printing press. As it turned out, experienced cutters could be found—many had emigrated to America—but artists remained in short supply. Winslow Homer saw his chance. What better way to earn his independence than to master this new craft for which there was so great a demand?

Resisting any temptation that he may have had to kick Bufford in the shins when his sentence as apprentice was over, Homer said goodby in the laconic, efficient, courteous manner he had cultivated. He hurried down the street to a studio he had rented in the Ballou Publishing House Building, home of the weekly *Ballou's Pictorial Drawing-Room Companion*, which boasted the then impressive circulation of over 100,000. He had made the acquaintance of a French cutter named Damoreau, who now taught him how to draw for woodblock reproduction. The technique carried him in directions quite different from those in which his Native School predecessors had been carried by their apprenticeships to other artistic processes.

Most of the Native School men had begun as engravers on metal. Metal, of course, can be incised with extremely thin, delicate lines which may be used to delineate small details or, by cross-hatching many small lines together, to capture subtle modulations of gray. Use of these modulations enabled the Native School artists to create the feeling of distance. On becoming painters, they naturally used a parallel technique, modifying their colors to make them indicate depth. As the eye penetrates the picture space of a Hudson River School landscape, the darks become lighter, the lights softer and less pronounced, until close to the horizon all contrast melts away. This method was well suited to expressing those deep vistas, symbolic of the huge American continent, which the Hudson River School loved to paint.

Homer's wood engraving process was incapable of such subtle modulations. Wherever ink touched paper the blackness was identical, with no variation in tone. Furthermore, the grain of the wood set a definite limit to the fineness of the lines that could be used to give the impression of gray. Homer could strike only a few crude notes on the black and white scale; he could imply distance only by showing far objects as smaller than near ones and by inserting obvious perspective lines, as when a long fence was made to cut obliquely from front to back.

In addition, the woodblock medium made it difficult for Homer to indicate rounded shapes. To fool the eye into accepting roundness, artists working in the flat must catch the delicate gradations from highlight in front to shadow toward the rear which exist on any three-dimensional form. The rudimentary nature of the gradations that could be achieved in the woodblock process prevented Homer from doing this, forcing him to visualize form primarily in silhouette. And, since the block could not reproduce subtleties of drawing, his linear effects had to be achieved with a few broad strokes. Yet the object of Homer's illus-

Three steps in making a woodblock illustration are shown here. First, the artist sketches the picture *(top)*. His drawing is then transferred to wood by another artist *(middle)*. In the final step, the block, often cut up into several sections to speed the process, is turned over to engravers who, working with a skill "as wonderful as the touch of the artist himself," carve out the wood between the lines—producing, according to the 1856 newspaper that ran these illustrations, "the most beautiful works of art without color that can be imagined."

trations remained that of the Native School—to give as full an impression as possible of three-dimensional reality. A wide variety of expedients was required. It is no wonder that good woodblock "designers" were hard to find.

Homer's style indicates that he was helped in solving some of his artistic problems by the consequences, oddly enough, of U.S. naval activity in the Pacific. Japan had been a never-never land to Western man until, when Homer was 18, an American fleet opened the islands to European trade. Along with a variety of other goods, examples of a great Japanese tradition of popular woodcuts journeyed across the oceans. The first of them to reach Boston and New York apparently arrived in the late 1850s. Making heavy use of silhouette, using firm lines and showing a refreshing indifference to conventional European notions of how pictures should be balanced, the Japanese prints were a liberating influence on Western art. In Paris, the prints brought into the practice of the most advanced artists—the American expatriate Whistler, that pioneer of Impressionism Manet, and others—many of the attitudes toward space and form which were being impressed on Homer's consciousness by his daily contact with the contrary and yet enchanting boxwood blocks. Homer surely was stimulated and encouraged by the Japanese prints to follow the paths down which his own experience was independently leading him.

All this training in a strange and difficult medium could not help but have an effect on Homer's later work. When he turned to painting he was not, like the Hudson River School men, used to dealing with the long perspectives made possible by engraving on metal. Instead, he employed strong, simple designs with comparatively shallow perspective. These remained characteristic of much of Homer's most mature work.

Woodblocks also influenced Homer's choice of subject matter. Since the method was incapable of achieving those deep sonorous vistas which the Hudson River taste required, he was forced in another direction followed by the Native School: toward those depictions of the behavior of ordinary people which art critics call "genre."

It was with a genre piece, done less than four months after his escape from Bufford's, that Homer made his first noteworthy appearance on the artistic scene. His second published woodblock was placed on the front page of *Ballou's Pictorial*, and the text accompanying his picture began with a statement that could not help exhilarating a youth whose previous work had been signed with his employer's trade name: this "local view" had been "drawn expressly for us by Mr. Winslow Homer, a promising young artist of this city" *(page 42)*. The view itself, representing the "Corner of Winter, Washington and Summer Streets, Boston," seems to explode on the page. From a short distance inside the picture a carriage is dashing madly at the spectator. If the horses are weirdly out of drawing, this attracts attention, and all the distortions are aimed at expressing diabolical speed. A lady carrying a parasol escapes destruction only by the hem of her voluminous skirts; and a gentlemanly policeman, who is raising an admonitory hand, is clearly as helpless as a rabbit trying to stop a snowstorm. The rest of the composition is crowded with picturesque characters, the left foreground being enlivened by an organ-grinder and his monkey.

The young Homer possessed to perfection that complete freedom of line, growing from an utter lack of pictorial inhibition, that is among the greatest gifts a humorous draftsman can possess. Ballou commissioned him to depict on the boxwood blocks life as it was lived in other parts of Boston. The editors also accepted a scene of country jollity, a cornhusking party in a barn *(page 43)*. Homer portrays with great gusto the rural custom of swains demanding kisses when they find red ears of corn. One young man gets a passionate response from a shameless maiden, another girl is in full flight, while in the center of the picture a triangle is acting itself out: a lad prepares to kiss one girl while another attempts to draw him back by his coattails.

During the same year that Homer escaped from his apprenticeship, *Harper's Weekly*, which was to become the greatest pictorial newspaper of 19th Century America, was founded in New York City. After the editors of *Harper's* had accepted some of Homer's drawings, the artist decided to make himself more accessible to this better market by settling in New York. The move carried Homer from an artistic backwater to the capital of the Native School. He took lodgings in a boarding house, but soon discovered that the leading painters worked (and sometimes lived) at one of two other addresses: the Tenth Street Studios and the old New York University building on "Washington Parade Ground" (now Washington Square). Homer moved into the University building, perhaps because it was less in demand (the Tenth Street building had its own exhibition hall and housed the artistic cream).

The University building was a monstrous relic of the old romantic taste, done in a bastard Gothic style. Morse, who had kept a studio there, had loved the building, which seemed to him a masterpiece of refined architecture. He had even painted it. But men of Homer's generation were unimpressed, although they found the studios useful. The novelist Thomas Bailey Aldrich commented after visiting Homer there that some buildings are gay while others "appear to suffer disappointments in life and grow saturnine. . . . The University is one of those buildings that have lost their enthusiasm. It is dingy and despondent and doesn't care." To get to Homer's studio, Aldrich continued, the visitor had to pass through "long uncarpeted halls" and up staircases which Aldrich found as mysteriously chilling as if they were haunted by tragic ghosts. Near the top, the visitor had to mount a little staircase as steep as a ladder to reach Homer's studio. There, however, all gloom vanished. In daytime, the sun poured in through Homer's one window—and at night the stars and moon were visible. Aldrich commented on "the splendid view" across the parade ground, over old treetops, down to where blossoms were "flaunting themselves." Homer's combination studio and bedroom was tiny—"it seems altogether too small for a man to have a large idea in"—but he was high above the city communing with his instructress, Nature.

The artistic society Homer now joined was altogether masculine and altogether good-humored. In those days there were no lady collectors and the few lady artists kept their distance. Many of the painters were, like Homer, unmarried, and those who were married left their wives home when they sallied out. Although drinking could be heavy and the artists dressed as they pleased, the atmosphere was not that of esthetes engaged in an esoteric calling but that of solid craftsmen working energetically together. One observer preserved a glimpse of Homer sitting on the model stand in his tiny room trying to finish a drawing that had to be in by midnight, while his friends laughed and cavorted around him. "Here, one of you chaps," he cried, "fill my pipe for me! I'm too busy to stop."

Homer was happy. Concerning his friends he wrote, "How I love these fellows." When *Harper's* offered him a lucrative job as a staff artist, he was not tempted. "I declined it because I had had a taste of freedom. The slavery at Bufford's was too fresh in my recollection. . . . From the time that I took my nose off that lithographic stone, I have had no master; and never shall have any."

Although residing in the capital of the Native School, Homer postponed his start as a painter while he continued his exploration of the possibilities of the woodblock medium. At first, he filled the shallow picture space with an irregular frieze made up of many characters—sometimes 40 in a single print—who were all engaged in occupations keyed to the central theme. As if he were throwing handfuls of confetti, he covered his figures with violently contrasting small patches of light and shade which, although they impede unity, create an energetic, nervous surface motion. Since subtle delineations of face and form would not reproduce, he engaged in gleeful caricature.

As the months and years passed, Homer achieved more power by advancing in every aspect of his drawings from the little to the large. He discovered that a few big contrasts of light and shade were more evocative than many small ones; he discovered that he could escape from caricature by synthesizing facial traits, poses and costumes into shapes so substantial that the blocks would reproduce them; he discovered that a few figures silhouetted against a background not too particularized carried more emotional impact than a reacting crowd.

With or without Japanese examples, Homer made an esthetic discovery that the Japanese prints were to bring into the art of the European Impressionists. Down the centuries it had been believed that in an artistic composition the forms on the two sides of a picture should be in balance so that, however much the forms might pull against each other within the picture space, the effect would be of an overall equilibrium. The notion that a picture could be lopsided and still have equilibrium did not come naturally to oil painters, who could elaborate where and as much as they pleased. The message was, however, hidden in the refractory and limited woodblock medium, since in woodblocks it was exceedingly difficult to make background shapes assume importance in the balance of the picture. It was natural for Homer, as for his Japanese predecessors, to ask himself what would happen if, by placing his foreground friezes of figures off center, he put much more "weight" on one side of the picture than on the other.

An outstanding example of Homer's success with this device is *Homeward Bound*, a print that calls to mind the bold designs of the French artist Toulouse-Lautrec (who, when Homer drew his picture in 1867, was only three years old). All the foreground figures are on the right side of Homer's composition; the only element that is beyond the center line is a lady's billowing skirt. These figures are gathered on the deck of a large boat: their weight would pull the picture down on the right were it not that various smaller forms, including a long strip of empty deck with nothing shown but the cracks between the boards, persuade the eye that the boat is rocking in the opposite direction. That the empty spaces are deeper than those that are heavily filled in gives them a compensating value in the design. The total result is not the static equilibrium that most artists seek, but a sense that the whole picture is rocking in the ocean that is dimly indicated far off on the left.

Americans in mid-century had become so fascinated with the look of their own world that Homer's modest—and, until the Civil War intervened, entirely nontopical—renditions of this world made him one of the most popular illustrators in the era's greatest news magazine. He depicted those aspects of local life that appealed to him. He showed America at play, sometimes children but more often young men and women of the right age for flirtation and courting. He much admired pretty girls. One of his friends remembered that when he looked in a store window and saw a pretty shopgirl, he would go in and buy some small item from her.

Homer has become so identified with the somber work of his later years, and elegance is so rarely thought of as a native American trait, that hardly anyone notices how gracefully he depicted scenes of mid-century pleasure in his younger years. The prettiest girls in the most fashionable costumes wander through rough New England fields with such enchanting daintiness that their sweeping skirts never catch in a bramble. They can even balance on rocks by mountain streams and fish with all the unruffled aplomb of countesses in a ballroom. Their young men are all handsome, energetic and perfectly groomed.

Homer was to become as dedicated a realist as the Native School produced. But his woodblock medium could only edge up to reality by legerdemain, and he was a young man, even younger in spirit than he was in years. Now that he had escaped from school and from Bufford's, he walked, as his own will dictated, through what may well be considered the golden age of America. When his youthful soul yearned for melodrama, he conjured up a slide of snow from a roof into a crowded city street. A pretty girl has been thrown to her knees and another is fainting delicately into the arms of her mustachioed swain, but the two wings of Homer's picture are crowded with spectators who find the mishap comic: it is perfectly clear that no one will really be injured.

So Winslow Homer fiddled in historic sunshine, ignoring storm clouds that were mounting on the horizon. The storm was to break as the greatest tragedy in American history: the Civil War.

One of Homer's strongest woodblocks is *Homeward Bound*, from the December 21, 1867, issue of *Harper's*. Not only does it convey a feeling of the rocking motion of the ship, but also, through its diagonals and receding lines, an unusual sense of depth for his work in this medium.

A Self-made Man

How did Winslow Homer become one of America's greatest painters? How, considering the fact that he had been brought up in Boston, then artistically backward, did he even manage to become the first-rate illustrator of magazines that he was before he began painting? What was the source of his single-mindedness? What compelled him, on his 21st birthday, to quit his drudge's job as an apprentice lithographer, and vow never to call another man boss again?

The answers are neither simple nor easy to come by: Homer abhorred autobiography, and he took great pains to conceal from the public what he tantalizingly referred to as "the most interesting part of my life." A cousin of his could say, "He got it all from his mother," but the cousin had only his artistic talent in mind. Surely his father's role had to be greater than such a statement would allow. Charles Savage Homer's failures alone—of which there were many—must have goaded his three boys to succeed, and succeed they did. But perhaps more important to the son who was making up his mind to become an artist was the father's untamable spirit. It had forced the older man to sell his hardware business and join the Gold Rush, only to return East minus his fine luggage and so broke that his patient wife had to pay his carriage fare home. And yet the elder Homer remained unvanquished. To the end of his long life he was a man to reckon with—and so, of course, was Winslow.

Photographs from the Homer family album show the baby Winslow propped up in a chair, his mother in fashionable dress, and his imposing if not always very effectual father. Winslow was the second of three sons.

Henrietta Maria Benson Homer

Charles Savage Homer, Sr.

Winslow Homer

Homework, 1874

Not the least remarkable thing about Homer is that he grew up having no master—unless of course his mother can be thought of as his teacher. She was working on one of her paintings not long before he was born, and her interest in art and in Winslow the artist continued right up to the end of her life. At an early age Winslow showed a precocity for drawing, and some of his childhood works still survive. Published here for the first time are two that contain seeds of his future work. The boy dreaming in the grass, drawn when the artist was 10, not only bears a close resemblance to the listless student in the later watercolor at left, but also seems to be the prototype of the barefoot scholars in *Country School* at right. The landscape next to the sketch, based on one of his mother's own watercolors, heralds Homer's rural scenes. But little does it suggest that one day Homer would achieve mastery in this medium and become one of America's most brilliant watercolorists.

Adolescence, 1846

Country School, 1871

Farmhouse, 1847

BALLOU'S PICTORIAL

M. M. BALLOU, { NUMBER 22 WINTER STREET. }   BOSTON, SATURDAY, JUNE 13, 1857.   { $3 00 PER ANNUM. 6 CENTS SINGLE. } VOL. XII., No. 24.—WHOLE No. 312.

CORNER OF WASHINGTON AND SUMMER STREETS.

The local view upon this page, drawn expressly for us by Mr. Winslow Homer, a promising young artist of this city, is exceedingly faithful in architectural detail and spirited in character, and represents one of the busiest and most brilliant spots in all Boston. The sketch is made from the north sidewalk of Winter Street. The most prominent building in the view is the large stone structure at the corner of Washington and Summer Streets, the lower story of which is occupied by the magnificent jewelry establishment of Messrs. Jones, Shreve, Brown & Co., and which vies in splendor and attraction with similar magazines in New York, London or Paris. This is always an attractive spot, and you can scarcely pass it any hour of the day without finding loiterers at the windows, with bright eyes gazing on the kindred diamonds, or scanning the superb plate, watches and rings there displayed in dazzling profusion. Within, the elegant arrangements, the spacious counters, the lofty groined ceiling and all the appointments harmonize well with the character of the business. Opposite this establishment is that of Orlando Tompkins, apothecary, which has recently been refitted and renovated in the style of the Renaissance, with carving, gilding, fresco-painting, mirrors, marble, etc., in the most approved style of luxury. We merely show the corner of this store. The name of George Turnbull appears upon the awning in front of his store, No. 5 and 7 Winter Street, which projected within our artist's field of vision. Turnbull's is another noted Boston establishment, and a fine specimen of the retail dry goods store. It is a favorite resort of ladies, who are attracted by the complete assortment of goods always found there, and the politeness and attention with which their wants are supplied. Mr. Turnbull enjoys an enviable reputation, and conducts a very extensive business. The figures introduced in our sketch, give a good idea of the character and bustle of this part of the city in the busiest part of the day. Here we have a carriage dashing up at rather an illegal rate of speed which might endanger the lady at the crossing, but for the gentlemanly policeman who is stationed here to ensure the safety of pedestrians and moderate the ardor of charioteers, and who steps forward to lend his assistance and interpose his potential authority. In another place we have an itinerant Italian with his organ, on the summit of which resides habitually a painful caricature of humanity in the guise of a monkey, attired in shabby habiliments, whose chief offices are to hold his hat for money and amuse the juveniles with his antic capers. Promenaders of both sexes, and pedestrians of all ages, complete the lively picture. At this point, Washington Street presents many of the characteristics of Broadway, New York. In the human tide that pours through it there is nearly the same diversity of feature and origin, and the amount of passing is perhaps larger in proportion to the size of the city, crowding the sidewalks full.

CORNER OF WINTER, WASHINGTON AND SUMMER STREETS, BOSTON.

Joseph E. Baker: *Portrait of Winslow Homer*, 1857

On his first and only full-time job, at Bufford's, Boston's leading lithographer, Homer looked as he does in the pencil sketch at left. "Fine as silk" was the way the co-worker who drew it described the dapper young man later. Once his two-year apprenticeship was over, Homer set himself up as a free lance and began drawing for *Ballou's Pictorial*, a weekly whose high moral tone made it safe to place "in the hands of the wife, the daughter, the son, or any within the sacred circle of home." His second published work appeared on the front page *(opposite)*, with appreciative comment, and among the many assignments that followed was the rambunctious cornhusking scene below.

But soon Homer was reserving his best drawing for *Harper's Weekly*. One of his liveliest contributions was the wood engraving reproduced on the following pages, in which a young swain wearing a handkerchief over his boater to protect his neck from the sun fearlessly frightens the ladies with a live lobster. But despite the delightful frivolity of much of his early work, there was no weakness or lack of resolve in the young artist. When *Harper's* editors asked him to join their staff, the independent Winslow turned them down.

Husking Party Finding the Red Ears, wood engraving, *Ballou's Pictorial*, Nov. 28, 1857

August in the Country—The Sea-shore, wood engraving, *Harper's Weekly*, Aug. 27, 1859

William Sidney Mount: *Music is Contagious*, 184

Jovial farmers were a specialty of William Sidney Mount, one
of the first American artists to record everyday life. As a painter
of "domestick, comick, or rural scenes," he established
the tradition of genre in which Homer did his earliest work.

III

A Home-grown Style

Homer's woodblock drawings of American life were high-spirited, devoted to the relaxations rather than the labors of the people, irreverent of pomposities and aimed at eliciting a smile if not an outright laugh. Toward the teeming streets with their wild horse-drawn traffic he reacted as would a humorous visitor from the country, emphasizing the pratfalls that lie in wait for the unwary in the city. And although he was now settled in New York, Homer still managed to find bucolic subject matter in the city's parks. All these preferences make it clear that Homer was strongly influenced by an established tradition of American art: the Native School approach to the scenes of ordinary living called genre.

During the late 1820s and early 1830s, shortly after Thomas Cole had introduced the Hudson River School landscape manner in New York City, genre had come into its own, also in New York. This second esthetic explosion was as revolutionary as the first, since genre, like landscape painting, was looked down on by the old guard of American art connoisseurs. According to their European-born esthetic theories, the correct method of depicting humanity was not genre but "history painting." History painters ignored their unexalted neighbors to recreate imaginatively the deeds of kings and heroes who inhabited a past considered to be more glorious than modern times; Allston, Morse and Vanderlyn, for example, had painted such ancient figures as Belshazzar, Hercules and Marius. This was a denial of both the democracy and the optimism of their native land, which found common voters admirable and looked upon the present as an era of great promise, when all of the evils of the past would be rectified.

As the 19th Century progressed, democratic concepts also made headway in Europe. Thus there was an environmental pull toward genre on both sides of the ocean. However, artists were timid in their approach to naturalistic scenes of contemporary living. Instead of painting the life around them, Europe's early 19th Century genre painters usually worked, as the history painters did, from texts. They were fond of illustrating homely or comic scenes from Shakespeare's

47

comedies or from Laurence Sterne's novel *Tristram Shandy* or from Cervantes' *Don Quixote.*

One of the first important American genre painters, John Quidor, following the Europeans, found his best subject matter in literature: Washington Irving's tales of a vanished Dutch New York. Quidor was an alcoholic artisan who made his living emblazoning images—half-naked Indian girls were much in demand—on the sides of the fire engines that volunteer companies pulled through New York's streets. He first displayed his characteristic style of painting in 1828, when he exhibited a scene from Irving's "Legend of Sleepy Hollow": *Ichabod Crane Pursued by the Headless Horseman.* Although color and form are exaggerated to convey terror, the picture reflects not fear of a dreadful unknown, such as appeared in equivalent European painting, but an American optimism. The action does not seriously involve the supernatural and is not truly frightening. The viewer of Quidor's picture, like the reader of Irving's text, is supposed not to shiver with horror but to rock with laughter.

Although as wayward in his technique as in his way of living, Quidor was an artist of great natural gifts. He offered an inspiration that others could fruitfully have followed. However, American genre painters did not stop at this halfway station. Instead, they turned from Quidor's transitional approach to a direct realism which was not to dominate European genre for another generation. In 1830, six years before Homer's birth, William Sidney Mount began to paint in the manner which the young Homer was, in many ways, to continue to practice.

Mount described the Long Island where he was born and lived, and where he found the subject matter of his paintings, as such "a delightful locality" that Adam and Eve would have preferred it to the Garden of Eden. No one labored in the Garden of Eden, and no one labored in Mount's genre paintings: the earth gave so abundantly that a man could fiddle away his days and yet eat well. Boys were always hilariously escaping from their chores. And when Mount painted two farmers bargaining for a horse he did not show comic yokels or sentimentalized peasants (as many European painters of the era would have done) but depicted solid citizens who were the leaders of their community.

In celebrating the life of his greater Eden, Mount felt no need to heighten or change reality: he became one of the most literal of genre artists. Like the painters of the Hudson River School, he sought to use technique to hide technique, to make the viewer feel he had actually been transported into an idyllic farmyard. To this effort, he brought dedication, charm, clear form and accurate observation of local color but no overwhelming power of expression or of imaginative identification. Mount's paintings are most likely to be loved by those most moved by his subject matter, which reflects the rural existence lived in the mid-19th Century by the vast majority of Americans.

Although their basic attitudes tended to duplicate Mount's, the younger genre painters did not form as coherent a group within the Native School as did the Hudson River artists. For one thing, they did not all congregate in New York City. Indeed, the greatest of the first generation, George Caleb Bingham, found himself artistically only after he had returned from the East to the Missouri where he had grown up.

Bingham's technique, although, like Mount's, largely self-invented, was much more concerned with what we would today call abstract values: he built his compositions, as if he were a precursor of cubism, on a few simple geometric forms. However, he hid his calculations so well that they do not obtrude and his paintings convey the Native School's characteristic impression of directly observed life. Bingham had two favorite subjects: flatboatmen engaging in high jinks as they floated down the Missouri River *(pages 58-59)*, and country elections. His election scenes are the ultimate expression of Jacksonian optimism. They portray what could have been the material for devastating satire—drunken voters, crooked and fatuous politicians—with the enthusiasm of an adolescent who boasts of a prank that is all the gayer because it is somewhat disreputable.

Perhaps satire would have been better, for it might have awakened men to the deepening crisis which eventually tore and almost destroyed the United States.

Like a house, full of confidence and the voices of children, that goes up suddenly in flames, so the American Elysium was engulfed by the Civil War. The memory still deeply scars the nation's spirit, even now when all the participants are dead. This was the nation's most terrible war, an agonizing fratricidal struggle in which the brother's sword was buried in the brother's breast.

Nor was the Civil War the only force that jolted American life in the mid-19th Century. An economic revolution, accelerated by military needs, overwhelmed the Edenic world which Mount and Bingham had so happily celebrated. Hordes of steam engines puffing from city to town changed the farmer bargaining for a horse from a leader of American life into a rustic relic; the leaders were now the presidents of railroads and the manufacturers of the goods that were flooding into general stores. These goods put the local artisans out of work; soon men who had lived by what they had created with their hands in their own workshops were forced to move to cities where they tended machines owned by plutocrats. Although in the end the Industrial Revolution would be tamed to American needs, it came ravening in like a fire-breathing dragon, darkening the skies with black smoke from iron nostrils. And whenever the smoke ceased, the result was disaster. The slaves of the machine, if put out of work by a depression, were more helpless than any Americans had ever been before.

Since genre painters were specifically concerned with the day-by-day behavior of mankind, and had indeed dedicated their art to celebrating those aspects of the American world now most threatened, the psychological and cultural foundations of their practice crumbled. In fact, only one artist of true vitality faced up to the problem in dark, desperate images.

David Gilmour Blythe had never shared the optimism of his contemporaries in the Native School, from whom, indeed, he was almost completely isolated. Even during the fortunate periods of his life, when,

A page from William Sidney Mount's journal, dated November 17, 1852, shows the artist's design for a horse-drawn studio and his enthusiastic assessment of its potentialities. The studio was actually built and fitted out with a plate-glass window. Inside were tables, drawers for storing paints, and a stove—the last enabling the artist to transfer a winter landscape to his canvas in perfect comfort.

as he put it, "hope was lined with velvet," he felt uneasy. His spirit was not attuned to happiness.

Born in 1815 to Irish and Scotch immigrant parents 40 miles from Pittsburgh on the Ohio River, Blythe was subject as a child to uncontrollable rages and unaccountable fears. When, having taught himself to paint, he traveled a smiling pre-Civil War countryside as a peddler of portraits, the likenesses he created showed little evidence of talent. Then, after a short period of married happiness, Blythe's wife died and the painter sank through descending spirals of alcoholism that alienated all his friends and left him alone in a world of psychic horrors. In this condition, he stumbled into Pittsburgh to discover around him a reality that echoed his nightmares.

Pittsburgh was a recent creation of the new economics. The city had no older traditions to temper the Industrial Revolution. It bellowed and blackened the air and degraded men. Then, as Blythe watched, the depression of 1857 threw thousands out of work. No one bothered with them now that the machines had no use for them. In the midst of poverty at its most dire, in the midst of the impersonal cruelty of man to man, Blythe's creative talent found wings.

He made obeisance to the dominant American genre tradition by casting his bitter homilies as humor. It was the humor to be found in a ragged urchin picking a rich man's pocket, or in a shoemaker laughing at a poor fellow who has brought in his last pair of shoes only to be told that they are past mending. Blythe saw the human race as made up of aggressors and victims: the aggressors are lank almost to the point of being skeletons but full of demonic energy, the victims squat and sluglike. When they meet in a courtroom, dominated by a devilish prosecutor, the victim is too sunk in degradation to come to his own defense, while both judge and jury doze in boobish unconcern with the tragedy being enacted.

Blythe worked all his life in back-country regions and remained ignorant of almost all sophisticated art, American as well as European. It is surprising that his technique, which combines self-invented felicities with the clumsiest naïveté, had the power to convey so much emotion. In emphasizing social satire, bitterness and pain—what 19th Century America called morbidity—Blythe was closer to the European than the American art of his time; it is too bad he was unable to study the work of Daumier, the great French artist who worked much in his mood.

O ptimism remained the accepted American note, even when so many of the reasons for the old optimism had vanished. The admired genre painters who were Blythe's contemporaries tried determinedly to hold on to the smiling mood of their predecessors. To achieve so difficult a goal they resorted to one of two expedients: either dispassionate factual reporting of a carefully selected scene or, if emotion was not to be avoided, a flight into sentimentality. Both expedients are well exemplified in the work of Eastman Johnson.

The son of a well-to-do Maine politician, Johnson studied at the German artistic center of Düsseldorf, at the Hague in Holland, and in Paris,

The Industrial Revolution threatened many innocent Americans with unexpected perils, as this moralistic cartoon was intended to show. Here two doe-eyed country girls follow the sign pointing the way to the great city—unaware of the pitfall at their feet, in which lurk the evils and temptations of urban living. Among these is a leering dandy in top hat, with the body and wings of a bat.

returning to the United States in 1855 with the best technical equipment of any American genre painter. Johnson's most famous canvas was a work he called *Life in the South* but which was rechristened (after the song) *Old Kentucky Home (page 60)*. This picture epitomizes how the genre artists were now stepping back from life. Although it shows slaves, the picture is so nonpartisan that it pleased people both in the North and in the South. The scene is laid in the slave quarters behind the house Johnson's father occupied as a government employee in Washington, D.C. Northerners could derive satisfaction from the clearly indicated contrast between the squalor in which the slaves were forced to live and the white world revealed by the elegant house against which the Negroes' rotting shack leans. But Johnson's adherence to the old genre tradition that emphasized not work but play enabled him to show the Negroes responding gaily to the banjo's sound. Southerners could note that the slaves were well-fed, unmarked by toil, picturesque in their rags.

When the War actually broke out, Johnson receded from reportage into sentimentality. In his *Wounded Drummer Boy* (which was so successful that he was called on to paint several versions), he showed a curly haired and seraph-faced lad, with one leg discreetly bandaged (no blood!), being carried on the shoulder of a burly soldier against a background of battle. The brave youngster is rallying his dispirited elders with his drum.

Most pre-Civil War genre artists, far from concocting such sentimental images, had gone the other way into an antisentimental raucousness. The boys in their pictures never pursued conscious virtue—they avoided work and loved mischief. Pictures of grown men often featured alcoholic prowess. But now, as American society became increasingly urban, the hedonistic freedom possible on farms began to fade away. Furthermore, the ladies now replaced the men as custodians of American culture. Dictating taste from drawing rooms where no fresh air was allowed to blow, they added refinement to sentimentality, creating a particularly noxious brew. High spirits departed from genre: an affected smile, a happy tear replaced the old horselaugh.

John G. Brown, the most financially successful exploiter of this taste —in a good year his pictures earned him $150,000 in today's money —was an immigrant from the Victorian England to which polite Americans now looked for refined manners. Brown invented a conception which glorified the new economics and justified the plight of the poor —the well-scrubbed newsboy.

Brown's newsboy, healthy and happy though clothed in rags, was pictured taking advantage of freedom of enterprise by ranging the city streets as an independent businessman. In some paintings he has a cute dog whom he teaches to do cute tricks, but it is clear that he will stop all such foolishness the instant an opportunity to make a penny comes along. Brown's newsboy, in short, is the opposite of Mount's shirking farmboy: mothers sentimentalized over him and businessmen could admire him as a hustler who would go far.

So strong became the taboo against paintings that showed indecorous

During a period of youthful study abroad, Eastman Johnson settled in The Netherlands, and there won for himself a reputation as the "American Rembrandt." Apparently Johnson never forgot the compliment. In this self-portrait, he is dressed as a Dutch 17th Century burgher. He later wore the costume to the Twelfth Night party at New York's Century Club.

behavior that when James Henry Beard and William Holbrook Beard, two brothers from backwoods Ohio, wished to continue in the old genre vein, they were forced to leave out human beings altogether and cast their pictures as animal allegories. They showed brown bears or dogs engaging in drinking parties or staggering home to be reproached by ninnyish wives. William even got away with depicting adultery by showing a rabbit surprising her mate under a cabbage leaf with another. The Beards' work elicited male laughter, and, surprisingly, praise from the most sophisticated American art critic of the time, James Jackson Jarves. Yet the Beards' wit and their muffled realism did nothing to stem the wave of sentimental refinement that had begun to wash over most paintings of American life by the time Winslow Homer felt ready to turn from his woodblocks to the oil and canvas of a genre painter.

However, the same forces that took the heart out of the Native School genre tradition strengthened landscape painting. As American society passed through war and economic dislocation, the gospel as God had written it in His fields and forests, hills and watercourses seemed ever more comforting, ever more inspiring. The Hudson River School became so dominant that one young American artist was surprised on reaching Italy to discover that the greatest paintings of the world were not all landscapes. Any effective landscapist could sell more views than he could paint and the leading artists became both wealthy and respected. Young men eagerly joined the Hudson River School. They found ready-made for them a successful, largely home-grown style which the Europeanized Jarves admired as "the thoroughly American branch of painting, based upon the facts and tastes of the country."

As the genre painters' belief in the nobility of everything American weakened, they increasingly turned to stylistic recipes brought from abroad. Nevertheless, the landscapists remained surprisingly immune to European influences even when they sought them. This is well exemplified in the adventures of John F. Kensett.

Kensett was a friend of the leader and chief theorist of the Hudson River School, Asher B. Durand and, like Durand, he secured his first training as an engraver. However, when he resolved to switch to painting Kensett concluded that he would do better not to experiment on his own but to study in Europe and absorb a sophisticated European style. For seven years, between 1840 and 1847, he shopped around abroad, settling at last on an English manner that involved painting restricted glades by crowding canvases with strokes of thick pigment. But no sooner was he home again, to see with a painter's eye American scenery and the work of his Hudson River School colleagues, than he jettisoned his English manner and swung into line behind Durand.

Another landscape painter, Worthington Whittredge, studied in Düsseldorf for some four years and then in Italy for another four. On his return in 1859, he was overwhelmed by the paintings he saw in New York. "Few masters of any age," he concluded, had surpassed Cole in "rugged brushwork." "When I looked at Durand's truly American landscape, so delicate and refined, such a faithful if in some parts sombre delineation of our own hills and valleys, I confess the tears came into my eyes." Deciding that "if I turned to nature, I should find a friend," Whittredge hid himself for months in New York's Catskill Mountains. "But," he mourned, "how different was the scene before me from anything I had been looking at for many years! The forest was a mass of decaying logs and tangled brushwood, no peasants to pick up every vestige of fallen sticks to burn in their miserable huts, no well-ordered forests, nothing but the primitive woods with their solemn silence reigning everywhere."

By seeking instruction before they had developed styles of their own, Kensett and Whittredge had sinned against the Hudson River School esthetic. Beginners, Durand had written, if they were not to sacrifice their individuality, should "go first to Nature to learn to paint landscape." Only after they had learned by themselves to imitate nature, could they "study the pictures of great artists with benefit." According to correct Hudson River School practice, artists should go to Europe only at a late stage in their development, and then not to acquire a style but to add refinements to a personal manner already established.

It took Whittredge years to get really in tune by discarding a persistent Düsseldorf quaintness and a formula caught from the German romantic landscapists, which caused him to leap suddenly from cool green foregrounds to hot pink skies. Kensett, however, having quickly abandoned his European manner, soon succeeded the aging Durand as the active leader of the Hudson River School.

Kensett shared with Durand the pantheistic belief that the purity of God manifested itself in natural beauty. They both tried to transcribe without editing the great visual hymns that rose from rock and tree. However, although Kensett, working largely after the Civil War, painted in more grievous times, he was the more serene of the two painters. He was less concerned than Durand with wild sweeps of distance that pull the imagination out over mountaintops. Instead he used mountains as backgrounds to wall in a safe world of pastoral delights. In his pictures tempests are friendly: the heart is less roused than at ease.

A s the 19th Century unrolled, artists everywhere became more interested in the painting of light. Kensett emphasized more than the older Durand the subtleties of outdoor illumination, which he captured in clear, lyrical color. However, he never sought the sharpest sunlight, the brightest hues. At a time when American life was clanging like a firebell, Kensett painted pictures so understated, so subtle, that a modern museum walker, used to more obtrusive art, must make an effort to pause and appreciate.

The majority of the Hudson River School painters practiced variations of the Durand-Kensett style, but within the school there was a dissident group more responsive to the clash and glitter of the times. These were descended from the other founder of the school, Thomas Cole, and, indeed, their leader was Cole's only important personal pupil, Frederic E. Church.

Like his teacher, but unlike most other Hudson River artists, Church read no healing gospel in the sunlit hills. The younger man found deeper meaning in the magnificent and mysterious workings of natural laws. He studied the physics of light and air, the biology of plant life and the geology of rock structures. As a painter, he sought to render landscape with scientific exactness, becoming even more eager, if possible, to achieve an accurate image than the members of the other branch of the Hudson River School who sought to express the visible word of God.

Personally, Church was possessed by a gargantuan energy that made him attack the problems of art the way a pioneer would attack the forest with an ax. At 20 he was already a leading painter who had demonstrated impressively the two esthetic concerns that were to dominate his career. On one hand, he was concerned with light; not Kensett's quiet radiance but light at its most dramatic. He would hang in his backgrounds the orange disk of a setting sun and show its almost horizontal beams casting deep shadows, striking the earth and water in contrasting brilliance, being reflected in a thousand different ways. He loved mist or smoke or even the dust thrown up by wagon wheels, anything that enabled him to catch an unusual light. His heroic orchestrations of light call to mind the wildly surging music of his contemporary, the German composer Richard Wagner. He may, in fact, have been influenced by written descriptions and black-and-white engravings (and perhaps even an actual example or two) of the work of the much older English landscapist, Joseph Mallord William Turner. However, he differed from Turner in his greater insistence on the solidity of earth. The Englishman felt that the sharpness and even the identity of forms could well be sacrificed to achieve greater effects of glowing air and light. Church, on the other hand, labored to show natural detail in all its attributes: shape, color, weight, texture, position, stillness or motion. In the exact, illusionistic reproduction of natural forms (which knowing European painters did not seek, preferring broader effects) he became probably as expert as any painter who ever lived.

However, by attempting simultaneously to pursue seeming opposites, he entangled himself in contradictions between the aerial and the solid, sky and earth, foreground and background—contradictions which it was the labor of his career to resolve.

Improved means of transportation and increased scientific curiosity about man and nature combined to make travel and exploration a rage in the 19th Century. Church became an artistic explorer, determined to distill on huge canvases the essences of the various exotic parts of the world. His *Heart of the Andes* summarized tropical South America; his *Cotopaxi* typified South American volcanoes; he sailed among icebergs to produce *Aurora Borealis as Seen in the Arctic Regions*; and finally, after more than 20 years as a professional artist, he went to Europe. However, he did not stay in the art centers of Western Europe, but instead explored regions then seldom visited: Greece and the Aegean, Egypt, Lebanon, Syria, the Holy Land.

Traveling usually in the summers, Church would spend a whole winter producing one of his vast geographic compendia. Each of his major pictures would, when completed, be put in the hands of a showman who would place it in a hall, surround it with suitable secondary decorations, and charge admission as to a theatrical performance. Crowds

Frederic Church's Olana—the fanciful villa he considered the center of the world —still stands on the heights above the Hudson. The artist designed the 25-room mansion himself, with some technical assistance from two of the country's leading architects. When asked whether the mansion indeed reflected his imagination, he replied, "Yes, I can say, as the good woman did about her mock turtle soup, 'I made it out of my own head.' " Even the patterns of the roof tiles engaged his interest—he made more than a dozen drawings for them.

flocked, not only in the United States but, after the pictures had crossed the ocean, in the great cities of Europe. Some London critics found Church superior to their own master, Turner, because the American combined effects of light and color similar to Turner's with "the most delicate and definite drawing, as well as a power of generalization which never becomes vague and careless."

When, years later, it became fashionable for American art critics to condemn as obviously superficial any work that appealed to the average man, Church's pictures, with their demonstrated ability to compete with theatrical shows, fell into ill repute. His art remains tremendously undervalued. In all his work, from small oil sketches made in the field to mammoth showpieces, he exhibited powerful vitality, glowing color, striking form. And consistently he narrowed the breach between light and shape, creating at the peak of his career some of the greatest romantic landscapes the world has known.

For some reason, Church never traveled to the American West. The exploitation of the scenic wonders of the Rocky Mountains, which were just then being opened to settlement and general curiosity, was left to an artist who was not considered by his contemporaries a member of the Hudson River School but rather as a Düsseldorf artist operating in America. This was Albert Bierstadt who had indeed been born near Düsseldorf and, although brought up in Massachusetts, had returned to Germany for instruction almost as soon as he resolved to be a painter. There he developed the meaty, picturesque manner of depicting peasants that he would later apply to Indian encampments: only a change of costume and the substitution of beer steins for tomahawks would be needed to transmute his braves into Westphalian farmers.

Because Bierstadt imitated Church's method of summarizing exotic scenery on large canvases shown for a fee, later critics have talked of the two artists in the same breath, but their practice was in fact very different. Where Church labored to catch the exact natural peculiarities of each region, Bierstadt blithely stated that the Rockies resembled the Alps and applied to them a dashing formula worked out not through observation but in his studio. Church's pictures are more impressive the more they are studied, but Bierstadt's are better at first glance, since he combined startling color contrasts, theatrical lighting and bravura passages of paint into images more eye-catching than profound. Yet, catch the eye they certainly do.

Although he was not truly a member of the Hudson River School, Bierstadt's art contributed to the triumphant popularity of American landscape painting. That popularity was to be seriously undermined in the latter part of the 19th Century by new esthetic movements coming in from abroad. However, the leaders of the Hudson River School continued to work and to sell late into the century, albeit to an ever smaller and older group of followers. But, all the while, Winslow Homer was reaching new heights with an art that combined the approach of the Hudson River men with the native genre tradition that had been laid down half a century before by Mount and Bingham and the other painters of that happier pre-War age.

William Sidney Mount: *Ringing the Pig*, 1842

For the People

The smiling work with which Homer began his career belongs to genre—that light-hearted category of art which shows ordinary people, like the farmers above, doing everyday things. It was only natural for Homer to have begun with genre. In the United States of his youth, the taste was for the direct rather than the subtle, for the illustrative rather than the esthetic. Genre suited a country busily discovering and advancing itself. There was still time enough left over for Americans to admire and laugh at themselves.

One of the remarkable things about early American genre before sentimentality gave it a saccharine quality is the durability of its humor. William Sidney Mount's *Ringing the Pig (above)* shows a familiar farmyard situation which produced chuckles in 1842—and it continues to do so, although times and viewers have changed. Like many another American artist of his day, Mount was largely self-taught, provincial, a man of the people. He began as a painter of signs and ornaments, and even at his most successful he rarely left the circumscribed world of his native Long Island, avoiding New York City and turning down several invitations to go to Europe. He had a democratic view of life, one that motivated other genre painters as well: "Paint pictures that will take with the public," he wrote, "in other words, never paint for the few, but for the many. . . . Some artists remain in the corner by not observing the above."

No detail was too minor for Mount to paint with a technician's care —like this sly hog from *Ringing the Pig (above)*. Slow to complete a work, Mount would often stop to prepare charcoal by burning grapevines, scour roadsides for natural earth colors and fire-test his pigments for durability.

George Caleb Bingham: *Raftsmen Playing Cards*, 1847

George Caleb Bingham did for the Midwest—specifically for Missouri—what William Sidney Mount did for Long Island: he recorded in a truthful and charming way the life he saw around him. He liked people, and people were always at the heart of his work. He did not see himself as superior to the boatmen playing cards on the raft drifting through a Missouri morning in the painting at left; he could have easily been one of them. Nor did he hold himself aloof from the high-spirited crowd receiving the news of an election in the painting below. Here, indeed, he was one of them: throughout his lifetime, he had an abiding interest in politics, and on occasion he even held public office.

A short, slight man, Bingham was by no means as unassuming as he looked. He was as quick to show his sense of humor as he was to speak his mind. Left completely bald by an attack of measles when he was 19, he wore a wig that on several occasions he employed to comic effect. Once he used it to startle a little boy, who later in life recounted the episode: "He arrived one evening for a visit, and I . . . was deputed to show him to his room. Filled with my own importance, I walked briskly ahead carrying a candle to light the way . . . and then lingered with childish curiosity. . . . After unpacking his artist's materials, he took off his coat and hung it on a chair, went to the bureau, untied and removed his choker, and then to my unspeakable amazement, lifted off the entire top of his head, exposing a great white dome. I was speechless with fright and fled in terror. . . . From that hour, Mr. Bingham assumed great importance in my eyes; for *me*, he was a marked man."

Bingham: *Verdict of the People*, 1855

Eastman Johnson: *Old Kentucky Home*, 1859

The honest gaiety of much American genre was tempered by the Civil War and the emergence of a moneyed class that equated art with status—but knew little about art. Sentiment was what the public wanted, and one of the painters who let it flow stickily from his brush was Eastman Johnson. The most famous of his early works is *Old Kentucky Home (above)*, actually painted before the War, but already redolent of the sweetness that would perfume such later productions as *Scissors Grinder (right)*. The painting presented so ambiguous a view of slavery that it found admirers in both the North and South. During the War, however, one Northern critic felt constrained to remark that the white mistress shown entering the yard no longer enjoys "the sport of the slave, but scowls through the darkened blind at the tramping 'boys in blue.'"

That Johnson could be a very good painter is attested by many of his later genre paintings, simple scenes of country life, such as *Winnowing Grain (opposite)*, in which he has captured the very quality of transient light. But he did not find the patrons for these he expected, and Johnson finally gave up genre altogether, returning to his first, more lucrative occupation, portrait painting.

Johnson: *Scissors Grinder*, 1870

Johnson: *Winnowing Grain*, c. 1873-1879

John Quidor: *Antony Van Corlear Brought into the Presence of Peter Stuyvesant*, 1839

John Quidor and David Blythe went largely
unrecognized in their own time, though both painted with
gusto and down-to-earth humor. Quidor's boisterous
imagination comes through in the painting above,
one of the many he based on the writings of Washington
Irving. The wildly gesticulating figure in the detail—
literally struck dumb by the blast of the trumpet
—is a Quidor invention, brought to life by the
impetuous work of the artist's quick, laughing brush.
Blythe's humor, by contrast, has bite. In the first of his
three paintings shown here, a bedraggled artist—Blythe
himself—returns home to find that he has been evicted for
nonpayment of rent; in the second, a rump-bumping
crowd pushes its way to a post-office window at its
own peril. The cartoonlike third picture offers a sharp
political commentary: Lincoln going about the fearsome
task of putting down the Southern rebellion, with one
leg shackled by his enemies in Tammany Hall.

Blythe: *Art versus Law*, date unknown

Blythe: *Post Office*, date unknown

David Gilmour Blythe: *Lincoln Crushing the Dragon of Rebellion*, 1862

David Blythe's humor was often rude, and perhaps this explains why he had so little success. William Beard, on the other hand, employed a time-honored method of painting the human comedy without offending anyone. He disguised people as animals. The bears at right certainly look like bears, but who has ever seen a big brown bear with a demure partner on his arm stopping to chat with a friend as one is doing at the center of the painting? And what is the reason for all this drunken merriment? These are none other than the bears of Wall Street celebrating a drop in the stock market. It remains unrecorded whether Beard considered a companion painting showing the bulls reacting to the drop.

William Holbrook Beard: *Bears of Wall Street Celebrating a Drop in the Market*, date unknown

IV

The Impact of War

Home Sweet Home, c. 1863

The Civil War, which was to change radically so many aspects of the American way of life, was also a turning point for the art of Winslow Homer, although the new direction his work would take was not immediately clear. When the conflict erupted, Homer was a regular contributor to *Harper's,* the era's greatest pictorial weekly newspaper. And he continued to do drawings for *Harper's* throughout the War, traveling to the front on several occasions to sketch the troops in battle and in bivouac. But suddenly, while the conflict was becoming more and more grave, Homer turned from his woodblocks and tried his hand at oil paints. Perhaps he made this new departure at long last because he felt the need of a more profound medium than woodblock engraving in which to capture the face of war. Whatever the reason, the change was not only sudden but permanent.

At first, it would seem, Homer was reluctant to go to the War at all. During his years as an illustrator, he had avoided news events, preferring those views of a relaxed and smiling United States that were also the subject matter of the genre painters among whom he had worked in New York City. And he remained loath, even as the guns prepared to speak, to turn away from play to the grim reality of bloodshed. He may have covered Lincoln's inauguration in March of 1861. *Harper's* published a large woodblock of the scene which, although it does not bear Homer's signature, appears to be in a style similar to his. It is an impressive picture, heavily shadowed and seeming to convey an atmosphere of brooding menace. In any case, Homer spent the first war summer of 1861 in one of his favorite haunts, rural Massachusetts. There his principal response to the War was that when he drew pretty girls he sometimes pictured them sewing for soldiers rather than flirting at a cornhusking bee.

Homer, always independent, refused *Harper's* offer to make him a war correspondent on the regular payroll. Yet he was finally drawn to the fighting as a free lance. It appears that he first went to the front in the fall of 1861: in its issue of December 21, *Harper's* published a picture by him called *Bivouac Fire on the Potomac.* Then, in the spring of

1862 he marched with the Northern armies on the abortive and bloody Peninsular Campaign, during which General George McClellan's forces laid siege to Yorktown but failed either to take the stronghold or to inflict crippling damage on the Confederate Army of Northern Virginia. The news drawings Homer sent back were published in the magazine almost every week. A typical title: *Rebels Outside Their Works at York-Town Reconnoitring with Dark Lanterns.* His *Bayonet Charge (pages 78-79),* so *Harper's* boasted, was "one of the most spirited pictures ever published in this country." The natural energy of his line, indeed, enabled Homer to depict with great effect the turmoil and violence of battle.

However, although he was to make several other trips to the front after the Peninsular Campaign, Homer seldom accepted assignments for which he had to report specific news events. He turned instead to scenes of camp life, of soldiers attempting to while away the boredom and loneliness of those long pauses between fighting which are a part of every war. Preferring as always to capture the universal rather than the specific, he filled his notebooks with drawings of army life in general which he worked up into finished pictures after returning to his New York studio.

Some of these drawings he used as the basis for woodblocks printed in *Harper's,* but his appearances in the magazine became increasingly rare, for in 1861 he set off on his new and exciting esthetic quest. Up till then his entire professional experience had been as a draftsman. Now, at 25 years of age, he decided to learn how to paint. The decision made, he pursued his new art according to the antipedagogical notions of the Hudson River School. The sum total of his formal instruction in oil paint was about five lessons on how to set his palette and mix colors, which he received from an obscure artist of French extraction, Frédéric Rondel.

Homer sketched Lincoln standing at the railway station with his son Tad and General Grant only a few days before the President was assassinated. The artist apparently redrew the scene for *Century Magazine* in 1887. No one knows why he omitted the President's beard.

Homer's first finished picture in oils was painted in his New York City studio from outdoor sketches he had made when with the Army in Virginia. It is a close-up of a sharpshooter, seated in a tree and firing at a target off canvas. In the tradition of native-grown American painters, Homer did not regard this initial effort as a student exercise to be tossed away after it had been succeeded by a better one. To a friend who watched while he painted, Homer did not speak about problems of technique; instead he speculated on how much money the picture would bring. After some debate he decided that he would not take less than $60, "as that was what Harper paid him for a full page drawing on wood."

The *Sharpshooter* completed, he painted a soldier serving out a sentence for drunkenness by standing balanced on an old crate with a log held like a gun over his shoulder. Then, not the least bit shy about these initial efforts, Homer put the two canvases in an exhibition. Indeed, he announced that if they did not sell he would give up his cherished independence and become a regular salaried staff member of *Harper's.* The pictures were both sold. Some years later Homer was enraged to discover that they had been bought by his brother Charles, whom

Winslow had told of his threat to join *Harper's*. Winslow was so angry that he did not speak to his brother for several weeks. However, at the time Charles's chicanery was successful and Homer was encouraged to go on with his painting. His second batch of pictures was snapped up without family intervention.

Homer's oils continued to sell and increasingly attracted critical praise. Doubtless especially pleasing to Homer (if he read it) was a sentence which appeared in a review in the *London Art Journal:* "These works are real: the artist paints what he has seen and known." Homer's paintings were also admired by his fellow American artists who, after Homer had been working with oils only four years, accorded him their highest honor—election as a full member of the National Academy.

This august body, which had been founded in 1826, possessed a handsome headquarters with its own gallery at Fourth Avenue and 23rd Street in New York. Although Homer was far from being what Dr. Samuel Johnson, the great English essayist, called a "clubable man," and was usually unwilling to talk art with other artists, he often attended Academy functions. He came to be regarded with affectionate humor by the other members as a crusty character. He was particularly known for his hatred of glass over pictures. In old age he would comment angrily that all he could see when he looked at a painting shielded by glass was the reflection of his own bald head. He remained fond of the institution and exhibited paintings at its annual shows during most of the rest of his life.

Until the time of his election to the Academy, Homer's oil paintings had dealt almost exclusively with the Civil War. He never visualized fighting as heroic, in the manner of the old, grandiloquent history painters. He showed, instead, a horror of carnage in the depictions of hand-to-hand engagements that he occasionally executed for *Harper's* and in the battle scenes he committed to his sketchbooks. These works express a deep pity not only for the wounded but also for the embattled men forced into committing such dreadful deeds. When transmuting his sketches into the heavier, more thoughtful medium of oil paint, Homer totally avoided, as if he could not bear to dwell on them, the desperate aspects of war. His closest approach to a battle painting, *Skirmish in the Wilderness,* is primarily a landscape with a few figures in the distance: its ominous effect is supplied chiefly by the gloom of the wood. In none of Homer's paintings which show military action is the enemy visible.

Homer's liking for unwarlike war scenes followed the prevailing fashions in genre painting. As a group, the painters of the Civil War sought, in the new genre manner, sentimental anecdote or factual reporting of the less grievous aspects of military life. In the old manner, they often glorified male high jinks.

Homer painted several pictures with sentimental overtones. The best known of these works shows two soldiers dreaming in front of their crude tent as they listen to a band in the background play "Home Sweet Home." However, by keeping the sad faces in shadow, by emphasizing (in his woodblock manner) costume and pose and

OUR SPECIAL.

Homer noted the light side of army life in a series of colored lithographs the size of playing cards, which he had a friend issue in an edition of 24. *Our Special* spoofs the artist himself, showing him wearing a goatee as well as a moustache. *The Guard House,* which later became the subject of one of Homer's oil paintings, takes a poke at troublemakers in the ranks.

THE GUARD HOUSE.

setting, Homer skirted the very edge of mawkishness and took refuge in Yankee taciturnity. The viewer of *Home Sweet Home (page 66)*, though spared a rush of tears to the eyes, is made to feel the depth of long-sustained loneliness.

Homer's ostensibly comic pictures of camp life only rarely elicit a real smile. *The Last Goose at Yorktown*, which shows hungry soldiers stalking a tantalizing meal, should be mischievous in the manner of Mount, but instead conveys desperation. And his seemingly factual reports of ordinary events carry disturbing overtones. Thus, a viewer seeing Homer's rendition of a bugler and two drummers sounding reveille does not need the military camp indicated in the background to tell him that this is not a peacetime event, but part of a grim, over-hanging tragedy. Already in these first, somewhat amateurish oils, Homer was revealing the gift that lay behind much of his subsequent greatness: without being summoned, his unconscious and half-conscious feelings welled out through every stroke of his brush, giving his pictures profound emotional overtones.

Homer was aware of this quality in his painting. Indeed, it was one of his firmly held beliefs about art (or at least his kind of art) that a painter's emotions would reveal themselves in a faithfully painted picture without the painter's having intentionally put them in. This conviction was the subject of one of his few (and characteristically terse) pronouncements about painting. Speaking to a friend who was an enthusiastic amateur artist, he said, "Gilchrist, when you paint, try to put down exactly what you see. Whatever else you have to offer will come out anyway."

As the Civil War dragged to its close, Homer began work on a canvas that seemed to sum up much of the waste and heartbreak of that terrible conflict. For weeks on the roof outside Homer's New York studio lived a "lay figure," a humanlike contraption of wood that could wear clothes and would hold any pose the artist desired. Day after day it stood in the sunlight, sometimes dressed in Union, sometimes in Confederate, uniform. The painting Homer was creating, which is called *Prisoners from the Front (page 80)*, came to enjoy a celebrity after the War similar to Eastman Johnson's *Old Kentucky Home* before the War began. Like Johnson's, Homer's picture was nonpartisan. It showed a dapper Union officer receiving, in sadness more than triumph, three Confederate prisoners. One is a Confederate officer, a battered but defiant remnant of Southern chivalry. The others, enlisted men, both look bewildered and one of them is elderly, far past the years when a man should be asked to fight.

Throughout his career, Homer tended to base his effects not on the revelation of character through emphasis on individual faces but rather on the essential humanity of total figures seen in their settings. However, in *Prisoners from the Front*, which he did not finish until after the Civil War, he came closer to the usual genre style of his compatriots, for he made considerable use of facial expression. But in other respects the canvas reflects Homer's customary practice, learned from his struggles with woodblocks, of concentrating on a frieze of figures

Innocents abroad, Winslow Homer and his friend Albert W. Kelsey pose together for a Parisian photographer. Homer sits upon the column, in an apparent attempt to disguise the fact that he stood only five foot seven. Kelsey, who inscribed the picture *Damon and Pythias* after the devoted friends and Pythagorean philosophers of the Fourth Century B.C., remembered Homer years later as a lively young man who enjoyed the gay life of Paris.

Homer loved dancing, and among the drawings he made for *Harper's*, based on his Paris experiences, are scenes of highlife at the Mabille dance hall *(left)* and the Casino. *Harper's* printed the pictures but appended to the drawing of the Casino a dour comment: "We shall not venture to look into the abyss on the brink of which these frenzied men and women are dancing, and this too curious crowd of spectators is treading. This is work for the severe and steady eye of the preacher and moralist."

in the foreground. A few other figures in the middle distance serve to keep the picture space shallow so that the viewer's eye is not distracted from the soldiers who supply the picture's meaning and emotional impact.

Examination of Homer's Civil War paintings shows that his self-invented method of laying on paint was both simple and straightforward—as it was to remain throughout his career. For better or worse, he never possessed what the novelist Henry James, in a review of Homer's work published in 1875, called the "secrets and mysteries and coquetries" of the brush. No one could yet have foreseen, looking at his early engravings and paintings, that as the years passed this young man, so much of whose experience had been in black and white, would become a great colorist. In these, his early labors as an oil painter, Homer began by trying to achieve brightness by placing independent patches of bright colors side by side on his canvases, as they were supplied by the actual view he painted, and by bits of natural or costume detail. When he realized that this fractured his compositions, he unsuccessfully sought harmony by sinking his palette into drabness. However, from the first he achieved strong effects of natural light. He worked broadly, as the lithographs and woodblocks had taught him to do, and somehow transmitted, despite his restricted technical means, a stupendous and original artistic gift.

In 1866, when he was 31, Homer made his first trip to Europe. Joining a friend, Albert Kelsey, also an aspiring artist, he settled in Paris where his *Prisoners from the Front* and another Civil War scene were hung in the American section of an important world's fair, the Universal Exposition. In this first post-Civil War year a number of young American artists traveled to Paris to shop for styles or to receive instruction. Homer seems to have had little contact with these compatriots and absolutely nothing to do with any of Paris' famous art academies. In fact, even more rigidly than his Hudson River School predecessors would have recommended, he appears to have held himself aloof from the art around him. Little record of his activities survives. He certainly went to the Louvre; he did a drawing for *Harper's* of one of its great galleries. But, characteristically, instead of emphasizing the works of art which that impressive museum had to offer, he put them in the far background and placed in his foreground two pretty girls who are engaged in copying pictures. The young ladies are idealized, but Homer made fun of the Bohemian costumes of several male art students, who scowl under their flowing locks with the most ridiculous concentration.

Had Homer been able to examine what Claude Monet was doing—which is most improbable—he would surely have been moved despite himself, since the young French artist's work contained startling parallels to his own. However, Monet and the other Impressionist landscapists had not as yet managed to display any significant amount of their work; their first group exhibition lay eight years in the future. The Academicians who still ruled French taste doubtless bored Homer, and the French nature painters of the Barbizon School were too remote from his interests to be of much concern. The Old Masters were old fogies. As for the Japanese prints that were on display at the exposition where Homer's own canvases hung, this renewed contact with Oriental art could only have encouraged Homer to experiment further with certain design techniques he had already tried. He appears to have made at least one experiment in the manner of Courbet, the French landscapist, but the fact remains that all the pictures in Paris seem to have interested him less than the city's streets and dance halls, which he also drew for *Harper's* (including a comic portrait of himself in one dance hall scene). After a stay of about 10 months, he returned to the United States, on the surface not greatly influenced, although many a felicity had undoubtedly sunk into his unconscious mind to reappear, when needed, as an aspect of his own vision.

Once the Civil War was in the past, Homer turned away from military subject matter. He did not wish to commemorate; he wished to forget. He returned with enthusiasm to the favorite subject matter of his antebellum woodblocks and of the native genre school: American country life. But he did not recede into coldness or sink into sentimentality, as did so many of the genre painters who were escaping from the disillusionment that had followed the War. He adhered rather to the attitude of the Hudson River School landscapists, who found happy inspiration in the fields and hills. A typical picture of the time by a conventional genre painter depicting a veteran returning home would have shown the noble young man catching a pretty sweetheart who has swooned in his arms while his tearful mother stands by. Homer's *Veteran in a New Field (page 83)* on the other hand shows a farmer sweating under a broiling sun as he harvests a field of grain with a scythe. The farmer's back is to the viewer, so that he need not be particularized and can stand for Everyman.

This painting carries, in the manner of all great art, as great a variety of overtones as does life itself. A viewer can feel simultaneously

Though for a while Homer turned from illustration to devote more time to painting, he resumed contributing to magazines upon his return from France in 1867—probably because he needed the money. He also did book illustrations, including this one, his interpretation of a passage in Longfellow's *Excelsior:*

"O stay," the maiden said, "and rest
Thy weary head upon this breast!"
A tear stood in his bright blue eye,
But still he answered, with a sigh,
Excelsior!

at least two reactions, one humorous and one more serious. The first is an amused pity for the poor veteran who has survived the War and returned home only to find he must immediately get on with the farm work. The second is a recognition that after the horrors of battle such a peaceful, if laborious, task cannot help but be a positive delight.

Since people and landscape were inseparable for Homer, each meaningless without the other and both essential to the mood, he was as much a landscape as a genre artist, and he showed his psychological affinity with the Hudson River School in many ways. He never painted city scenes, preferring to stage his art in the countryside. And he traveled widely, as the landscapists did, in search of novel subject matter. Of course, the discoveries he prized were different from those that appealed to painters of pure landscapes. He had no interest in a waterfall that a man could contemplate but over which he could not paddle a canoe. A mountain brook lacked appeal unless there was a fisherman standing in the middle of it casting for trout. Homer always wanted a scene of human action.

Homer's heart was in his native New England. To idealize what he saw there seemed to him unnecessary, superfluous, even blasphemous: he lovingly painted rocky fields, crumbling stone walls, barns that had grown rickety while presiding over generations of healthful labor. And his farm girls, as they carry a bucket of milk or hold a pitchfork in front of a haystack, are universalized in loveliness as the memory universalizes youthful passion. Of course he painted small boys, those favorites of the old genre artists: boys clumsily clad but engaged happily in wild games like snap-the-whip; or two boys crossing a pasture, the older stalwart, the smaller one timid, yet both imbued with the beauty of the time and place.

Homer's gift was to catch the eternal moment—not a generalized view but a single instant that epitomizes an aspect of the universal. In the old Hudson River School manner, he hid his own personality, appearing to make no comment, and thus the emotion of the picture seems to grow entirely from its subject matter. For those post-Civil War Americans who were reacting violently against American life, Homer's resolutely American subject matter threw up roadblocks to appreciation. Henry James, on the verge of deserting America for England, complained that since Homer's work portrayed America, it was doomed to be ugly. James wrote:

"Before Mr. Homer's little barefoot urchins and little girls in calico sun-bonnets, straddling beneath a cloudless sky upon the national rail fence, the whole effort of the critic is instinctively to contract himself, to double himself up, as it were, so that he can creep into the problem . . . . [Homer] is almost barbarously simple, and, to our eye, he is horribly ugly; but there is nevertheless something one likes about him. What is it? For ourselves, it is not his subjects. We frankly confess that we detest his subjects—his barren plank fences . . . his flat-breasted maidens, suggestive of a dish of rural doughnuts and pie. . . . He has chosen the least pictorial features of the least pictorial range of scenery and civilization; he has resolutely treated them as if they *were* pic-

Henry James expressed contempt for Homer's pie-nurtured farm girls, while his own fine stories and novels had American women as heroines. Nevertheless, he did find American scenery and manners graceless and, shortly after penning his devastating appraisal of Homer, he settled in England where, among ancient buildings and customs, he felt more at home. This contemporary sketch shows the author in 1894, when he was 54.

torial, as if they were every inch as good as Capri or Tangiers; and, to reward his audacity, he has incontestably succeeded."

Much of Homer's work did picture, as James put it, "the national rail fence." But there was another, more elegant side to Homer's art; if he loved farms and barns, he also loved summer resorts, those haunts of the well-to-do. Himself a natty dresser, Homer had a keen eye for fashions and he frequently painted young ladies, tripping like huge, brightly colored, oddly shaped birds across his foregrounds, their ribbons and voluminous skirts blowing in the breeze. When he represented them on the beach, he sometimes showed a stretch of leg, a clinging of wet cloth to curves, that critics considered immodest, yet he always kept his distance. His pictures express an admiration for pretty girls, untroubled by the lust to possess.

The wilderness, that domain of the founders of the Hudson River School, came into Homer's art relatively late, but then it came with a passionate rush. Not until the late 1870s did he add to his repertoire the masculine adventures of hunting and fishing in the north woods. The delay may have been because nature's wildness did not have for him, as it had for Cole and Durand and the other Hudson River School men, a romantic gloss. He saw instead savagery, hardship, an appeal to the stoical fortitude of wild animal and of man. This only became meaningful to him as his view of the world darkened appreciably in his middle years.

It was contrary to Homer's whole approach to art to paint primarily from the imagination, to show effects which his eyes had not seen. On the other hand, this quiet-seeming man had a romantic passion for the extraordinary. Increasingly spurning commonplace effects, Homer was forced to engage in long and patient searches for the exact subjects he wanted. A friend wrote that his purpose was to find "the rare or exceptional phase of nature, and especially the dramatic, and to reproduce with fidelity and power the effect waited for or discovered." Having sought out Nature in her most beautiful or most striking moods, Homer then sought to conjure up the technical means that would enable him to express what he saw. Thus he reversed the usual procedure of educated artists, who first learn technique and then find subject matter to which it can be applied.

By necessity, therefore, Homer was always experimenting, searching as he painted for the means to express what he saw. These experiments soon carried him so far from normal Hudson River School practice that he was proceeding largely on his own. Yet, surprisingly, his development matched in many ways that of the most knowing group of artistic creators of his generation: the French Impressionists, 3,000 miles away.

Like these French innovators, Homer sought to convey a moment's impression in the eye and mind. This was a revolutionary concept both in America and abroad, since academic 19th Century artists, like most of the greatest painters down the ages, put into a picture not only what could be seen at a moment of time but also what the mind knew to be there. A conventional figure painter, for example, reproduced all the buttons on a coat although a glance would reveal only that the coat was buttoned. This had been true of landscape artists as well. The great Dutch landscapists such as Jacob van Ruisdael had included as much detail as they could in their meticulous canvases. The Hudson River School men carefully painted every leaf and blade of grass in their foregrounds, and Frederic Church crammed into one of his great landscapes a whole encyclopedia of scientific lore.

When such artists recorded more than the eye could normally see, they were forced to work laboriously in their studios, elaborating the effects of light to convey their complicated message. The evanescent qualities of outdoor illumination could, at best, only be approximated. However, Homer was, like the Impressionists, determined to reproduce open air vision. By the late 1870s he had come to perceive clearly the effects produced by natural light. In a statement worthy of the most radical of the Impressionists, he explained his theory to G. W. Sheldon, a contemporary writer on art. "You have," Homer said, "the sky overhead giving one light; then the reflected light from whatever reflects; then the direct light of the sun; so that, in the blending and suffusing of these several luminations, there is no such thing as a line to be seen anywhere." Homer set out to capture such evanescent "luminations" as well as to record what the eye saw—no more and no less—in a fleeting instant of time.

This was an extremely difficult task, putting a great strain on Homer's technical equipment and on his artistic ingenuity. One problem with which he continued to wrestle was the fact that nature by no means can be depended upon to cooperate with the artist in the matter of color. A maple tree, its leaves turned flame red in the autumn, may look fine next to the dark green of a fir. But painted on a canvas, their violently contrasting hues may clash, destroying the unity of the work of art.

In struggling with this difficulty, Homer reached quite different solutions from those achieved by the Impressionists. In a manner arising from the sophisticated traditions of European art, the Impressionists struck a prevailing color note in each painting and established around it a unity of tone. But Homer did not choose to adopt an expedient which, for the sake of harmony, would inevitably involve the artist in slight modifications of the actual colors in nature. As a result he did not use color with the charming delicacy characteristic of the Impressionists. Instead he used it with power—and found unity within his canvases by other means. The old American School expedient for achieving unity had been a heavy reliance on black and white values, which the artists had learned from their experience as engravers. Homer now made this reliance his own. "It is wonderful," he said, "how much depends upon the relations of black and white. . . . A black and white, if properly balanced, suggests color." One has, indeed, to look twice at the few paintings Homer completed altogether in black and white to realize that they have no color.

To his delight Homer found that if his values were right—that is, if his colors balanced and harmonized in weight and intensity—he could use the most violently contrasting hues without fracturing the unity of his painting. A daring and successful early experiment in this area was *Croquet Scene*, in which Homer painted two ladies in frocks of brilliant red and blue against a background of bright green grass. Somehow Homer's painting holds together despite the vividness of the strong colors.

Homer also made great strides in his efforts to paint outdoor radiance. As Henry James admitted, he "naturally" saw "everything at one with its envelope of light and air." He had formerly been forced to keep in shadow those foreground forms which he wished to mute; now he learned how to use the dazzling effect of sunlight as a means for generalizing shapes. He also learned that aspects of light and atmosphere could be used, often more effectively than background shapes, to keep the viewer's eye from penetrating deeper than the painter wished into his picture space. But it was all a great labor, the more so because the evanescent effects he observed in nature would vanish before he could catch them in oil.

In this continuing quandary, his first teacher, the woodblock medium, which he still occasionally used to help eke out a living, came to his rescue. Since the technique of the cutters had improved, enabling them to indicate a subtler range of values, he increasingly supplemented the line drawings he made for them with a gray watercolor wash. From this it was only a step to creating watercolors in full color.

Homer became seriously interested in watercolor painting in about 1873. Although for some years he did not use the medium freely, he achieved almost at once several delightful results. His watercolors came so rapidly that he could sell them for low prices, and they sold so readily that he was able to lay aside his illustrating. More important, they enabled him to capture elusive outdoor effects that would previously have vanished before he could record them.

The art galleries of Homer's youth usually crowded paintings on the walls all the way to the ceilings; artists spoke grimly of having their works "skied." To make matters worse, glass was often put over paintings, causing reflection, and the major illumination came from skylights, as in the Art-Union Gallery at right. Homer once facetiously suggested to the director of the Carnegie Art Institute in smoky Pittsburgh: "You know you can always get light by taking the soot off the glass on your roof."

Now his watercolor practice became the pathfinder which his oil practice lumberingly tried to follow. He would spend whole summers sketching in watercolor. Thus in 1880 he stayed with a lighthouse keeper in the middle of Gloucester Harbor in Massachusetts, hunting the multiple effects of light on water. His catch was brilliant, paralleling (as Homer's biographer Lloyd Goodrich points out) the work being done at that time by such Impressionists as Monet, Pissarro and Sisley. However, when Homer got back to his easel and tried to do the same thing in oil paints, his hand failed him. He found this extremely discouraging.

The eternal experimenter, Homer was also engaged in a second nerve-racking labor. When he had first taken up oil painting he had, in his quest for realism, lost the fastidiousness, the grace of his woodblock designs. Yet there remained a side of his nature that called again for decorative elegance. To a painter of a different kidney, this would have been easy to achieve: one needed only to imitate any of a thousand tried and accepted formulas. But Homer was determined to achieve felicitous composition without the slightest retreat from his own personal vision or from naturalism. Toward that end he made considerable strides, but still it seemed to his eager mind that his oil painting lagged. The brush would remain for disheartening hours motionless in his hand, or he would angrily scoop out with his palette knife what he had achingly painted.

To make the strain worse, his critical reputation was showing distressing fluctuations. Most reviewers were friendly, but few showed the enthusiasm that had greeted Homer's work in earlier years and many revealed a lack of comprehension of what he was attempting to achieve. The oils sold slowly, and frequently for a good deal less than Homer's original asking price. In 1879, for example, Homer priced three oils at $1,500 each and not one sold. When he had started out as an oil painter, he had worked closely enough to the established taste to be almost immediately successful: admirers of the Native School automatically admired him too. But he had left that established taste behind as he had moved toward his own American brand of Impressionism. And the New Taste that was arising around him was inimical to all he was trying to do. The post-Civil War generation of critics and connoisseurs despised everything American and believed that the point of a picture lay in those very "coquetries" of the brush Homer consciously and determinedly avoided.

Outwardly a brusque Yankee, Winslow Homer always tried to give the impression that he cared nothing for the opinion of critics, or of anybody else. But, like most Yankees, he was a good deal more vulnerable than he liked to pretend. And as a supremely honest artist he was doubly vulnerable. He was not a facile craftsman creating pleasing images. Instead he was struggling with great intensity to discover the technical means to render in paint exactly what he saw. Thus he was putting his very being on the line every time he painted. Any rejection or neglect is very painful for such a man—and Homer was entering some painful years.

The Declaration
of the Eye

When Homer came to New York to free-lance for *Harper's*, he was struck not so much by the art he saw around him as by the smell of paint in the galleries. It was an alluring odor, and it re-awakened in the young magazine illustrator from Boston his desire to be a painter. Boldly he set about producing his first oils, scenes of the Civil War that concentrated more on camp life than on the violence which fills a wood engraving like *Bayonet Charge (opposite)*. It was peace, not war, that really interested him, and even before hostilities ended, he turned to the tranquil subjects that would preoccupy him for the next 15 years—the country and the farm, girls and boys, pretty women and the seashore, warm and happy and safe under a summer sun.

Trusting his eye to tell him what was right, Homer struck out on his own. He went directly to everyday life for his material, made studies under the sky, sometimes even painted entire pictures outdoors. And soon he was filling his paintings with a natural radiance and a brilliance of color never before seen in American art—and comparable to the work of the French Impressionists. Looking at these early oils, it is hard to imagine that this man who liked so much to be in the thick of things would one day turn his back on it all—his painter friends, the healthy, good-looking people and the land running over with thick green grass—to retire to a lonely corner of Maine and paint a furious, sullen sea.

Bayonet Charge from the July 12, 1862, issue of *Harper's* seems to put Homer in the thick of battle. Actually he saw little combat as an artist-correspondent, and of some 20 paintings he based on his war experiences, only five show action.

Bayonet Charge, wood engraving, *Harper's Weekly*, July 12, 1862

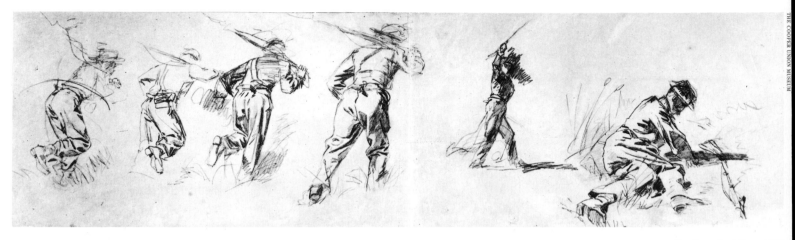

Studies of soldiers, 1863

Sketch of cavalry soldier, c. 1863

The most famous of Homer's Civil War paintings is *Prisoners from the Front* (*below, left*). Finished after the War, perhaps from on-the-spot sketches like those shown here, it portrays victor and vanquished in a dispassionate light. Its style is still basically that of an illustrator, straightforward, with an emphasis on line. Yet the prisoners have been painted with subtlety and a depth of characterization surprising in one so new to the brush and oils. Only the face of the rifle-bearing guard, in its square-jawed simplicity, recalls a stereotype Homer worked out for himself in his wood engravings. The painting's lasting popularity eventually became for the artist a cause of concern. "I'm sick of hearing about that picture," Homer complained when critics who failed to understand his more mature work referred to it wistfully in their reviews.

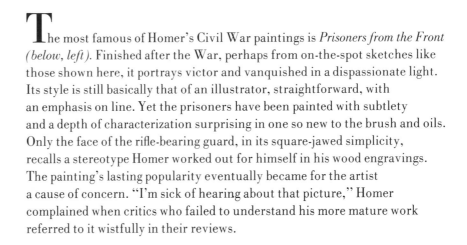

Sketch of buglers, 1862

Prisoners from the Front, 1866

Spring, date unknown

Homer marked the War's end with a peaceful painting —*Veteran in a New Field (top, opposite)*. This was among the first of many pictures he would do of farm life, such as the wash drawing above showing a family beside a well, or the nostalgic oil painting of a boy "nooning" on the lawn *(right)*, in which once again there is an echo of that childhood drawing, *Adolescence (page 40)*. These were the unpretentious, down-to-earth subjects that attracted Homer. To him they represented a stability sundered by war and industrialization, and he painted them with such longing that he gave to them the freshness of morning. An artist friend, John F. Weir, remembered how Homer's delight in the seemingly insignificant once manifested itself on a visit to the home of Weir's parents: "He went with me to West Point and enjoyed it, even to the pleasure of looking out from his bedroom window over the vegetable garden toward the barn at sunrise; I can recall the tone of his ejaculation—'Just *look* at it!' "

Veteran in a New Field, 1865

Nooning, c. 1872

Another of Homer's favorite subjects was women. He painted girls with such great admiration, not only for their beauty but also for their clothes, that his paintings constitute a record of changing fashions in the post-Civil War era. Though he was always a stylish figure, and carried himself in a way that impressed people, there must also have been something shy about him,

Hunting for Eggs, 1874

a distance or remoteness that never allowed women to get really close
to him except for those within the relaxed circle of the family. One
woman who had come to know him on picnics could sum up her
impression of Winslow Homer years later in a single sentence: "He was
a quiet little fellow, but he liked to be in the thick of things."

Autumn, 1877

Summer, 1874

Upland Cotton, 1879-1895

On one of his many trips away from his New York studio, Homer ventured South, there to renew his acquaintance with a world he had discovered during the War—that of the American Negro. He became so absorbed that he returned to Virginia several times, and from these trips came the bright paintings reproduced here, two of the half dozen he did on Negro themes. He painted the ex-slave with rare sympathy, and more than once got into trouble for it. An offended belle asked him, "Why don't you paint our lovely girls instead of these dreadful creatures?" "Because," said Homer, "these are the purtiest." On another occasion he was threatened with bodily harm; local toughs were determined to get rid of the "damned nigger-painter." One of them advanced on the porch of the hotel where he was sitting. The artist did not retreat; he did not even get up: "I looked him in the eyes, as mother used to tell us to look at a wild cow." In the tension of the moment, a Texan sitting nearby sought refuge under a bench, but still Homer did not budge. Both hands in his pockets, he stared the intruder down—or at least that is what he thought he did. Later the Texan offered Homer his explanation of what really had happened—"He thought you had a derringer in each hand."

Carnival, 1877

87

Berry Pickers, 1873

The sea that one day would dominate Homer's late work began to have a place in his paintings as early as 1873. He used it, however, more for its reflected light than for the power exploding through the stormy seascapes of his last years. For Homer the genre artist, the sea was still largely a pleasant background against which he could show children berrypicking, seesawing, sailing. And out of his celebration of innocent themes like these, there again came to him a flurry of critical acclaim. One writer who praised his work for its "sense of freshness and pleasureableness" was moved to say of the man himself, "He paints his own thoughts—not other persons'."

What were the thoughts that Homer was attempting to paint the summer of 1873? He had found a new interest in watercolor and was using it, as in the first two pictures above, done at Gloucester, Massachusetts, to set down his impressions of light and color. But he seems to have been after something else as well. The third painting is not a watercolor but an oil. In the light washing through it, and in the broad, fluid handling of the paint, it reveals the degree to which Homer was letting watercolor affect his thinking about oil. Three years later he employed a watercolor done in 1873 as the basis for one of his most beloved oil paintings, *Breezing Up (right)*. Some of the spontaneity of the original was lost in the transformation, yet a real breeze is blowing here and, more important, the sun beats down, permeating even the shadows with its radiance. Homer was pleased with the results. However, when a friend asked to buy the painting, the artist wrote back telling him not to. "I am about to paint much better pictures," he explained.

Breezing Up, 1876

See Saw, 1873

Children on the Beach, 1873

V

Esthetes
and Expatriates

Winslow Homer's paintings increasingly failed to please the taste of
post-Civil War America because that taste was changing—and changing
largely for the worse. Mark Twain, in a book he wrote with Charles Dud-
ley Warner ridiculing the boom era that followed the War, derisively
called the period the Gilded Age. The name has stuck. It was a time
when war-stimulated industry underwent explosive growth, when the
pursuit of power and wealth flowed so strongly through the veins of the
adolescent nation that greed appeared to have become the country's
dominant emotion. Just as green valleys disappeared under heaps of industrial waste, so the old American idealism seemed to disappear under
avalanches of money. Virtually all government control lay in the future. Giant companies were formed and ran rampant over the land, cor-
rupting officials and squeezing out small competitors. Clever (and often
crooked) stock market manipulators could make vast fortunes over-
night. Money was amassed by the bucket, the barrel, the boxcarful,
until—so it was reliably estimated—some 10,000 New Yorkers had an
untaxed income of more than $100,000 a year (some $500,000 in buy-
ing power today).

Although the underpaid working people were being victimized by
these Robber Barons, as the worst of them were later called, there was
at first little social protest. The American commonality felt for the plutocrats less resentment than admiration. If a poor man were young, he
could hope some day to be a millionaire himself. If he were old, he
could dream that his children would make the climb. There was wonder rather than envy in the voices that whispered, as their owners
passed Mrs. John Jacob Astor's house on New York's Fifth Avenue, that
her bathtub was "cut out of a solid block of marble" and weighed two
tons. And what a delightful vindication of American democracy it was
when Mrs. William K. Vanderbilt (whose forebears were less than illus-
trious) forced Mrs. Astor off her plush high horse by giving a ball cost-
ing $250,000 (more than one million dollars in modern money) from
which the haughty Mrs. Astor could not bear to stay away!

Unlike the modern rich, who generally try to hide their wealth, the

A love of the sea translated into
paint yielded Homer one of his
most powerful oils, *Lookout*.
Washed by moonlight, the
seaman cries out, "All's well,
lights all up," as the ship's bell
reverberates to the ancient call.

Lookout—"All's Well," 1896

plutocrats of the Gilded Age did everything in their power to show it off. A family's most conspicuous public symbol, of course, was its house. Fifth Avenue soon groaned under mansions, each built in one (or more) of various elaborate styles borrowed from the Old World. The apex of the trend was celebrated in a poem by Wallace Irwin, a popular writer of the time:

Senator Copper of Tonapah Ditch
Made a clean billion in minin' and sich,
Hiked fer Noo York, where his money he blew
Buildin' a palace on Fifi' Avenoo.
"How," sez the Senator, "can I look proudest?
Build me a house that'll holler the loudest—"
. . . .
Forty-eight architects came to consult,
Drawin' up plans for a splendid result;
If the old Senator wanted to pay,
They'd give 'im Art with a capital A.
. . . .
   Pillars Ionic,
   Eaves Babylonic,
Doors cut in scallops, resemblin' a shell;
   Roof wuz Egyptian,
   Gables caniptian,
Whole grand effect, when completed, wuz—hell.

The wealthy did not stint on the insides of their houses either. Every Gilded Age parlor was crammed: as a writer on interior decoration pointed out, a room could not be considered overcrowded as long as it was possible to move around in it without knocking things over. The plutocrats naturally had to own more things than anyone else, and costlier things as well. For these expensive objects they looked to Europe —and this included paintings.

The patrons of the Native School, who had been actively concerned with developing an American art, had usually grown up in the middle of the American landscape. When they had become successful merchants, they had continued to deal personally with local storekeepers across the land. But the plutocrats' eyes were raised above the land; their magic involved the manipulation not of assets but of paper that stood for assets; they had little contact with ordinary American life. And their wealth made them seem in their own eyes to resemble less their own compatriots than the nobility, past and present, of Europe. What they wanted they bought: they would buy European nobility.

The best way, of course, was to marry a daughter to a duke, but that could not always be managed. The next best way was to buy European culture. Collecting Old Masters was temporarily out of style and so the plutocrats bought the same kind of contemporary pictures that were being bought by the most "correct" European collectors.

It should not be imagined that the canvases that then flowed into America are now enshrined on museum walls. If museums actually own the sort of pictures the plutocrats bought, the examples now repose in

All that money could buy in 1882 is represented by the William K. Vanderbilts' three-million-dollar mansion which once dominated the northwest corner of New York's Fifth Avenue and 52nd Street. Built of stone imported from France, the home had stained-glass windows and a two-story banquet hall, above which there was a gymnasium.

their cellars. The names of the artists: Baugniet, Toulmouche, Détaille, Lefebvre, Berne-Bellecour. Their work: expertly finished genre costume pieces, decorative or sentimental or learned or spicy, illustrating literature, exotic climes or aspects of the past.

If an American plutocrat bought the works of American painters, he wished them to resemble such imported confections—a discouraging trend for artists such as Homer who were still faithful to the ideals of the Native School. To judge by his notes to his dealers, Homer was always profoundly disturbed when his work did not sell. He did not regard painting, as other artists were then doing, as something so refined and precious that it was not for the common herd. Like the Hudson River men before him, he painted pictures for the people to enjoy, to please the eye of the common man. When his works did not please, were purchased slowly or not at all, he underwent periods of anguishing doubt.

Many other American painters were assailed by a different doubt, a doubt that the United States in the Gilded Age could have anything whatsoever to offer the artist. Shocked by the Civil War, ill at ease with the growing materialism of subsequent American life, they felt alienated from their own world. They saw nothing around them that they wished to express. The landscape in which the Hudson River School reveled seemed to them raw under bright American sunlight, crude in its lack of age-old habitations. With the novelist Henry James, they considered American civilization the least picturesque that had ever existed. With James, they went to Europe; several, again like James, became expatriates.

The patron saint of the new movement was an American-born painter, two years Homer's senior, who had spent only a few years in America and never returned there after settling in Europe in 1855 at the age of 21. James Abbott McNeill Whistler even denied having been born (as he was) in the industrial town of Lowell, Massachusetts: "I shall be born when and where I want, and I do not choose to be born in Lowell."

As an art student in Paris, Whistler had heard the French painters who were his friends rail against the bourgeois culture of France, a culture that had its resemblances to the American Gilded Age. Mingling his own feeling of rootlessness with a general scorn for the materialistic mid-century middle class, Whistler became a prophet of the doctrine of "Art for Art's Sake." Art, he contended, was entirely independent from, and much superior to, everyday life. A work of art had no connection with the environment in which it was produced and no meaning apart from its beauty. Subject matter was therefore of no importance; all that mattered was how the painter rendered it. Whistler explained the title of the canvas he called *Arrangement in Gray and Black* by stating that it could be of no possible interest to anyone but himself that the picture showed his mother. The lasting popularity of "Whistler's Mother," as the painting is almost always called, would seem to prove that the artist, despite his theories, was deeply moved by the human significance of what he painted.

Since the doctrine of Art for Art's Sake was a determined turning away from a society that the artists found tasteless and alien, Whistler

Surrounded by a covey of stuffed doves, Mrs. William K. Vanderbilt models the Venetian gown she wore the night of her housewarming ball. She and her husband spent an estimated $250,000 to make the party the most magnificent ever given in the United States. Rooms were flooded with roses, palm trees were decked with orchids and the costumed guests quaffed champagne all night long.

lost no opportunity to make a show of his professed hatred of the bourgeoisie. He cultivated an arrogant, cutting wit and dressed in an outrageously dandified manner. Paradoxically, he engaged in such she- nanigans that (like Salvador Dali today) he kept himself constantly in the hated public's eye. His extravagant behavior prompted the French painter Degas to say, "Whistler, you behave as if you had no talent."

However, Whistler was bursting with talent and refused to be limited by his own theories. He pontificated that "Nature is always wrong," yet his beautiful and delicate "symphonies" and "arrangements" and "nocturnes" are poetic impressions of specific aspects of the actual world. When mist-softened factory chimneys called to his imagination medieval bell towers, the two images fused recognizably in the resulting picture. Although he professed to scorn environment, he put down roots (as did Henry James) in the old capital of the English-speaking world, London. For anyone familiar with Whistler's work, it is impossible to walk along London's Thames embankment on a foggy day without hav- ing the master's ghost shift the scenes before his eyes.

After the Civil War, American artists followed Whistler to Europe in a flood. Unlike their predecessors of the Native School, they jour- neyed as rank beginners with no professional careers behind them. This was to a considerable extent a result of the times: the machine economy was weakening the artisan pursuits in which American painters had tra- ditionally been nurtured and from which they had absorbed their prag- matic approach to art. Where the members of the Native School had gone to Europe to improve their self-taught styles, the new students went to Europe with empty hands, seeking altogether new departures.

The first Mecca for Americans was Munich, where a school of paint- ers had developed a style then much in fashion. The Munich artists began by covering their canvases with a rich brown base that would show through the overpainting, thus giving their finished pictures the time-darkened appearance of Old Masters. Then, with a champion fenc- er's agility, they slashed on other colors, achieving with energetic brushstrokes a bravura effect, startling if not profound. In its insistence on the artist's virtuosity, this Munich style was the very opposite of the self-effacing approach of Homer and the Hudson River School.

Hardly had the first Munich students brought their dashing manner back to the United States than the star of Munich set in the interna- tional art firmament. Americans had to go elsewhere because they could not be behind the times. Some went to Belgium or Holland, but the vast majority gravitated to Paris, the city that was finally establishing itself as the art capital of the Western world.

In France, the Americans were caught up in a long-drawn-out peda- gogical system much of which dated back to the 17th Century. They had to draw from plaster casts and then from the nude model until they could reproduce every part of a human body in any conceivable posi- tion. The use of oil paint was a separate step, as was the composing of several figures, nude or clothed, into a logical picture. At the end of the road loomed a work equivalent to the thesis of a modern Ph.D. candi- date. The young artist combined what he had learned into his "Salon

Picture," an elaborate composition which was sent, after it had been approved by the professor (whose name would appear in the catalogue beside the student's), to France's official annual exhibition, the Salon.

The Americans worked with such concentration and obedience that they often won the school prizes. But few intended to stay abroad as Whistler had done. They regarded themselves as esthetic missionaries who were preparing to carry back to their native land valuable gifts that would at long last establish a worthy art in what they thought of as an artistically barren desert. That their gifts, being brought from outside, might not be applicable to the expression of American life, did not concern these younger painters in the slightest. They wanted to have as little contact as possible with American crudities—and did not the doctrine of Art for Art's Sake demonstrate that art demeaned itself if it had traffic with nonartistic life?

These students hoped, of course, that after their return to the United States they would sell their works to the plutocrats who had been importing pictures. However, shrewd businessmen preferred to acquire the real thing from Europe rather than imitations being created in their own cities by their own compatriots. Although the old Native School had enjoyed an enthusiastic local market, "the Younger Men," as the members of the new generation continued to be called until they were elderly, had great difficulty selling their canvases. Painting ceased to be a lucrative profession in America. Yet the Younger Men did get control of the critical media: the art magazines of the era sang their praises in shrill choruses which Winslow Homer must have found very annoying. Many a name reverberated much louder than his in the contemporary ear. Some of these men—like W. T. Dannat and Robert Reid—are now all but forgotten. Others are only well known to those especially interested in the history of American painting, including John Twachtman, J. Alden Weir and William Merritt Chase.

Even so simple a device as a soda fountain presented a gorgeous challenge to designers of the Gilded Age. This quasi-Gothic structure was exhibited during the Philadelphia Centennial of 1876 under the name of Minnehaha—"Laughing Water." Bedecked with flowers and adorned at the top with a vial-enclosed nude, it became one of the most popular displays at the fair.

One difficulty was that the new movement, and even the careers of the individual workers within it, could achieve little stability because the artists equated originality with practicing the most up-to-the-minute European fashions. Their esthetic world was in perpetual turmoil as each year's batch of students brought home new ideas and techniques. The Munich style was trodden under by arrivals from Paris, and then there was a succession of Parisian developments. If he were to keep afloat, a painter had to be adept at learning new tricks.

Take, for example, the career of the New Yorker J. Alden Weir. During the 1870s, while still under the spell of the conservative academician Gérôme, his Paris teacher, Weir stated that Manet could not draw and that landscapes by the French Impressionists were "worse than the Chamber of Horrors." Yet in the early 1880s, he began to imitate Manet's figure pieces and by the end of that decade the influence of out-of-doors Impressionism showed clearly. If not original or forceful, Weir's work has the charm of graciously assimilated culture pleasingly displayed.

The acknowledged leader of the Younger Men was Chase. Although Chase had started farther back on the path than Weir—he had been a Munich man—he subsequently followed a similarly meandering stylistic course. Far from reacting against the eclectic clutter of possessions sported by rich Americans, he used taste to do the same thing better. While Homer's studio was a bare workroom, Chase's was crowded with shards from every culture except his own. This hodgepodge, in the midst of which he received both his pupils and society ladies, was considered "of immeasurable service to American art." And it did do something to widen horizons. But the true contribution of the Younger Men to their society was as teachers: they brought home much technical wisdom which became extremely valuable as it was assimilated. Chase taught at New York's Art Students League, the famous and still-existing school founded by the Younger Men, and at several other places.

As a general rule, a painter's development reflects his growth as a human being, moving from youthful lyricism through maturity to mellow or feeble old age. But Chase's art was not enough of a personal expression to follow this biological flow. Typically, when he took on a new style he did not discard the old but added it to a continuing repertoire. He practiced all his styles with an awe-inspiring virtuosity. Each picture, whether a portrait or an interior or a landscape, circles around a single prominently stated effect of color or shape, expertly and elaborately orchestrated to fill to the edges a canvas often impressively large. Again and again the viewer feels Chase's personality fighting to express itself, but almost always it seems to get smothered under the technical virtuosity. His most emotional pictures are those he painted during old age in the style of his youth. With flashing Munich brushstrokes, Chase depicted dead fish whose cold but expressive faces communicate pugnacity, futile anger, macabre despair *(page 114)*.

The Younger Men, with their elaborate European training, brought to American art a technical expertness in the painting of the human figure, an area in which native skill was sadly lacking. Figure painters in the U.S. had mostly created genre, and genre painting (with the exception of Homer's work) had fallen on bad days. But when the Younger Men turned to landscape, the situation was altogether different. America possessed an active landscape school which supplied a native impetus that could not be ignored. The members of the new movement usually did not attempt landscape until late in their careers, and the landscapes they finally produced were more American in inspiration than their other work.

The new movement, indeed, produced no landscapist who was considered even by its own adherents comparable to George Inness. An almost exact contemporary of Frederic Church, Inness had been born into the high Hudson River School generation. He never completely lost his links with that school, although he brought to American landscape art a much more subjective approach to nature.

Inness was born with "a fearful nervous disease." Even had he wished to work in the full Hudson River manner, he would have been barred by his epilepsy and its attendant mental phenomena. The emotional control that enabled Church to complete his enormous, factually accurate canvases was impossible for Inness whose esthetic reactions tended to surge into his brain like explosions.

Inness first learned conventional European landscape formulas from a conventional French artist resident in America. Then he turned to the Hudson River School: "There was," he wrote, "a lofty striving in Cole, although he did not technically realize that for which he reached. There was in Durand a more intimate feeling of nature. 'If,' thought I, 'these two can only be combined. I will try!'"

In his twenties, Inness inaugurated the habit of making trips to Europe during which he shopped around for artistic inspirations that chimed with his own vision. In Italy, he was greatly impressed by the formal, noble, idyllic views of nature created there during the 17th Century by the expatriate Frenchman, Claude Lorraine. In England, he stood in awe before the naturalistic landscapes of Constable, and the more poetic renditions by Turner. But all these workmen spoke from the past. The most immediate European influence on Inness was exerted by the Barbizon School, which had arisen slightly later than the Hudson River School and occupied a roughly equivalent position in French art.

Barbizon was a village near Paris. That the French school was, like its American counterpart, named after a locality in which the artists worked reveals that its style was also developed to depict a specific corner of the earth. However, the views on which the Frenchmen concentrated were very different from the Hudson River School's rough and rugged Catskill Mountains. The Barbizon region was made up of small forests, neat meadows and little pools—a miniature, bijou world where the vistas were restricted, the objects few. Furthermore, the French painters, led by Corot, reduced the complexity found in the natural scene by generalizing with their brushes. To Hudson River taste, the pictures were no more than sketches. How could one take seriously, an American critic asked, a picture in which "a swamp and tree" constitute "the total sum"?

But Inness was himself addicted to meadows and worried by elaboration. Furthermore, he was moved by the fact that the Frenchmen's summaries of nature were essentially subjective: the Barbizon canvases were avowedly not renditions of landscape exactly as it appears but man-made commentaries on nature. And to top it all, they were unashamedly colorful—the Barbizon painters were enabled by the sophistication of their technique and the subjectivity of their approach to build their pictures more basically with color, the emotional component of painting, than the Hudson River School ever had succeeded in doing.

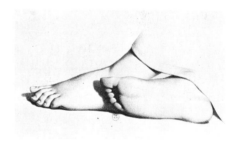

The diligent American art students who studied in Paris in the later decades of the 19th Century not only sketched plaster casts and living models but also improved their draftsmanship by copying drawings like these by Bernard-Romain Julien. Drawings by Julien were among those that Homer's father, thinking to encourage his son's artistic leanings, brought back in 1854 after a trip to Europe.

It was a revelation! Yet Inness was too imbued with Hudson River self-reliance to imitate the French style. What the Barbizon School did was to free his personal spirit from "fetters." Now he had to rush home and use what he had discovered to express his own reactions to his own land.

And so, after his return to the United States in 1854, he wrestled, in the manner of his fellow American landscapists, with his personal spirit in the presence of nature. His spirit called more passionately than those of his colleagues for untrammeled self-expression, but he was too close to the Hudson River School to want to submerge the facts of nature in poetic representation. He wished rather to

Homer displays a new English suit bought in 1880. Always a natty dresser, he wears a subdued tie and straw boater, and carries a walking stick. Most of his clothes were selected at Brooks Brothers in New York; over the years he amassed an enormous wardrobe and even at Prouts Neck bought a new pair of trousers every month.

merge the images of the inner and the outer eye into a single image.

By the mid-1860s, Inness had found his first mature style, and it brought him great acclaim both from artists and from the collectors of the Hudson River School. The problem of foreground detail he often neatly avoided by selecting views that began with a meadow. In his pictures complicated shape does not appear until the middle distance where the eye generalizes naturally. His greatest variation from normal Hudson River practice was in the use of color. The School tended to make color, however charmingly rendered, grow from form, but for Inness it was the soul of the picture, the winged emissary of his own emotion. Inness was to go on to other styles, but it was already clear that a great colorist had appeared in American painting.

When, after the Civil War, Inness continued his trips to Europe, he found himself surrounded by those artistic travelers who were to be known as the Younger Men. However, his attitude was never theirs. The practice of technical tricks for their own sake, he stated, showed that the painter "was not one with his subject." While the Younger Men boasted of their teachers, Inness still insisted that he was self-taught. Yet he was determined to work all new technical discoveries into his personal style. More and more he made color the soul of his pictures, capturing the effects of outdoor light, as he does in *A Pool in the Woods* *(pages 26-27)*. More and more he painted nature as the eye sees it in an inspired glance. Nevertheless, he disapproved of the way the shadows that mold form and create a sense of distance were sacrificed by the French Impressionists to brilliance of hue. Monet, he wrote, created a "pancake of color" that was a travesty on three-dimensional nature.

"Long before I heard of Impressionism," Inness wrote, "I settled to my mind the underlying law of what may properly be called an impression of nature." Although generalization was required, "the objective fact" (so dear to the Hudson River School) should not be muted but used to "elevate to a higher idea." It was necessary to reveal "that logical connection of parts to the whole which satisfies the mind. The elements of this, therefore, are solidity of objects, and transparency of shadows in a breathable atmosphere through which we are conscious of spaces and distances."

Although Homer would have grunted with distaste at talk about elevating "to a higher idea," this statement is broad enough to include the work of the Yankee genius. Inness had, in fact, defined what such modern critics as Lloyd Goodrich and John I. H. Baur have called Native American Impressionism. This point of view even affected those younger American artists who loved the work of Monet and acknowledged themselves his disciples. Only very rarely does an Impressionist landscape painted by an American fail to indicate its nationality: the American landscape tradition shows through in a greater concern with logical depth and the position of objects in space.

In taking Inness to their hearts, the Younger Men—who would admit no virtue in the older American Native School—ignored Inness' own explanations to proclaim that he, like they, had been made in France. But no one could claim that Homer had been made in France.

Stressing energy rather than refinement, his style shouted that it was home-grown. Furthermore, his subject matter offended the new taste. Correct genre painters either depicted models tricked out in exotic costumes, or, if they nodded toward American life, elegant ladies and uncomfortably washed children idling in the drawing rooms of the wealthy. Homer had an aversion to drawing rooms, and the children he painted were vigorous farm boys too busy with their work or their play to be overly clean.

Although Homer's work became less and less popular, he did not try to curry favor with the Younger Men or the critics who praised them. He had no use, he stated, for "those symphonies and queer things" by the god of the new movement, Whistler. The tendency among the returned students to burble about "beauty" so annoyed Homer that he would sometimes insist that his pictures were not intended to be beautiful. While he scornfully dismissed the esthetes, he mourned that "the average man" lacked "the comprehension of art" to sympathize with what he was trying to do.

However, Homer's uneasiness, his new feeling that he was out of joint with the world, was caused only in part by changes outside himself. He had kept a youthful lyricism, a boyish joy in the things of the senses, long past the age when this fine springing fades away in most men. Yet the years moved for him too, and now the time had come when he needed to express matters more profound and complex than light and air, the prettiness of girls, the mischievousness of boys and the pull of a sunny sail on a windy bay.

As emotional confusion began to trouble the man who had always painted high-spiritedly, the brush in his hand began to falter. This uncertainty, it is true, did not affect his watercolors, in which he was concerned only with recording his instantaneous reactions to nature. But his oils, which should have synthesized his experience with the deepest emotions of his subconscious mind, refused to coalesce. He began to suffer from an artist's most deadly ill: esthetic frustration.

So troubled did Homer become that he found it harder and harder to associate with his fellow human beings. A magazine writer noted in 1879 that "Of Mr. Winslow Homer's movements in summer-time no person however intimate . . . [knows] the secret." He was thrown into an agony of embarrassment when admirers came to call at his studio. The presence of his fellow artists bothered him, particularly if they showed an inclination to comment on his pictures. He even warded off members of his own family. Once when he knew his father was coming to call he hung a sign reading "COAL BIN" on his studio door to confuse the old man and keep him away.

Finally in 1881—he was then 45—Homer resolved that he would depart from everything and everybody he had ever known. He would try to work out his problems in utter isolation.

He sailed again for Europe, but not to any artistic Mecca. Instead of living in Paris, or even London, he settled in an English fishing village called Cullercoats on the North Sea, near the town of Tynemouth. There he rented a cottage with a garden surrounded by a high wall. For two seasons he rarely opened the gate to any knock. Living completely alone, he cooked, he washed the dishes, he swept (for in such matters he was meticulous), he drank (he always consumed a good deal of alcohol) and, above all, he wrestled, hidden there from the eyes of the world, with his artistic difficulties.

Homer had been drawn to this hideaway by the subject matter the region around it offered. Several summers before he sailed for Europe he had visited members of his family in Maine, where his financially successful brother Charles owned a house and land on Prouts Neck, a rocky promontory jutting into the untamed ocean. There he had watched the human race battle with the fierce sea. This primordial aspect of man's struggle for existence appealed to his deepest feelings—but in America he could not break his long-established habit of painting the smiling things, although they no longer served his temperamental needs.

Homer had traveled to a part of the Northumberland coast famous for its shipwrecks. At the head of the River Tyne, which flowed from the mining center of Newcastle, Tynemouth presided over a vast coming and going of wind-powered colliers. Outside the harbor, the heavy coal ships had to traverse a region of the North Sea that was haunted by cataclysmic storms. When nature raged, Homer would watch from the cliffs as the endangered vessels, carrying as much sail as they dared, tried either to beat their way out into the open sea or to navigate into safe haven behind the harbor's breakwaters. Too often they could do neither. Too often they were slammed by gale and breaker against the offshore reefs.

When this occurred a cannon would sound, giving the alarm. Homer's new neighbors had met the perils of their stormy coast by organizing lifesaving brigades; as the painter watched fascinated, hardened rescuers in oilskins would launch themselves in small boats into the towering breakers.

Homer perceived that he had a new, impressive and vivid subject matter that called for a deepening of his style. Temporarily laying aside his oils, he sought solutions in the more flexible medium of watercolor and, painting on an outsized piece of paper, achieved the most dramatic scene he had ever attempted, the *Wreck of the "Iron Crown"* *(page 104).* The three-master going to pieces on the rocks, the lifeboat with oars outstretched, driving toward it through the surf, the great waves—all are firmly drawn. And Homer washed in the ominously luminous white spray, the gray sea and the grayer sky with an impressive and moving freedom.

Homer also became fascinated with painting the women of Cullercoats. On ordinary days in the village no men were ashore, all of them having pushed off to sea in their fishing vessels by the gray light of dawn. When Homer issued from his gate, he walked through a world of women—but how different from the American girls who carried pails of milk or played croquet were these "fishergirls," as Homer called them. They were built for hard labor. They mended nets, gathered mussels and, if storm clouds rose suddenly, they watched from the cliffs, with the stoicism of the ages, as their men maneuvered the little boats toward the safety of the shore.

In depicting the Cullercoats fishergirls, Homer, for once in his career, borrowed from other men's art. This exception was the more remarkable because the influences he bowed to came from backward painters whose objectives were very different from his own. Instead of crossing the Channel and examining the work being done in Paris, Homer studied the styles of such English figure painters as Edward Burne-Jones and Sir Edwin Landseer. Their practice was the antithesis of Impressionism and of Homer's naturalism. They loved to particularize detail and they generally painted not real people doing real things but idealized figures: knights in armor, semihuman dogs, or allegorical ladies with superhumanly sweet faces. Much of their work was intolerably sentimental.

That Homer sought outside help indicates great need. Nothing in his experience had prepared him to depict the Tynemouth fishergirls with integrity. Sentimentality, which contrasted pretty faces and rough clothes, femininity and hardship, crept into the vacuum. His lack of true response made it easier for him to accept the contrived compositions, the artificial patterning of poses (arms, for instance, all held at the same angle), which he believed gave his art a formal structure it had lacked. The striding heroine of his *Inside the Bar* stems less from observation of life than imitation of an idealizing art. Among the few oils he painted in England was *Hark! the Lark (page 103)*, a work featuring three picturesquely accoutered fishergirls looking upward, which might almost have been painted by any one of many "correct" genre artists.

Yet the heavy atmosphere of the North Sea, the gray-blue water so rarely lit by the sun, brought to his work a new richness of tone, a new depth of color harmony. The pictures Homer brought back to the United States late in 1882, and those he created shortly thereafter from his English sketches, appealed more than had any of his previous work to the critics who represented the new taste. Here were renditions of transatlantic subject matter that resembled, to some extent at least, what one saw in European galleries. A lady reviewer, using the French word for watercolors, expressed her pleasure that Homer had accomplished "something quite different from the fresh and individual but crude and unpoetic suggestiveness of his earlier *aquarelles.*"

The temptation was plain for Homer to see. He could continue to paint in his new-found manner and please both the critics and the public. But Homer was not an artist who could repeat himself. He had discovered a more profound subject matter and was feeling his way toward expressing it. This breakthrough could only stir him to push his experiments further. His English experience did, in fact, prove to be only a short prelude to a new era in Homer's artistic life. Before him lay the great oils in which he would show, with ever greater power, men battling against the immeasurable and inexorable sea—and then the powerful late paintings in which he would capture as no other artist ever had the awesome majesty of the sea itself.

The Perilous Sea

Homer had told a friend in 1876 that he was about to paint "much better pictures," but these did not in fact come without trial. His inclination was to re-examine himself, to make a fresh start, leaving familiar things behind. And this he did, going abroad to a small fishing village on the English coast. His stay there launched a revolution in his subject matter: the sea rushed into his work, and the sun that had shone brightly in his earlier oils dimmed as wrecks and rescues became his dominant themes. Children vanished from his paintings, women changed from fashion plates into heroines (*opposite*), and men battled the ocean for a living and often for their lives. Nature, once regarded so benignly by Homer, suddenly was a force in his work, testing, it would seem, his mettle as a man as well as an artist.

When he returned to New York, he had passed the halfway mark in his career and a choice lay open to him. He possessed the means for achieving financial success —a more polished style, a flair for the dramatic. He could refine these elements, or he could develop still further the masculine robustness of his art—a quality that might offend polite Victorians. His choice was inevitable: on the very threshold of becoming a popular artist, he retired to Maine, to a barren promontory jutting out into the ocean. For Homer there would be no painting down to the crowd—"Winslow," said his sister-in-law Mattie, "hated a lie."

Three sturdy maids of Tynemouth pause in their labors to listen to the song of a lark. The painting, somewhat studied for a Homer, nevertheless approaches that quality Victorians desired most in art—finish.

Hark! the Lark, 1882

Nature as it confronted Homer in Tynemouth was neither smiling nor sunny. Under dark, moist English skies, he awakened to the drama of the sea as he watched the struggles of fishermen against an elemental force so much greater than they. But a curious aspect of his manly work of this period is the absence of men in it. When they do appear—as in *Watching the Tempest* and *Wreck of the "Iron Crown" (bottom, left)*—they are little more than huddled forms, anonymous in their oilskins. Women, on the other hand, dominate the Tynemouth paintings. Homer must have found the type alien at first: they were big-limbed, strong, capable of doing all the work delegated to them, including unloading the catch, taking the fish to market, mending nets and reprovisioning the boats. But Homer recognized in them a quality he admired—their forbearance. He applauded one such stalwart woman in *Coming Away of the Gale (right)*, in which she is shown with a baby strapped to her back, striding toward that protector of the lives of Tynemouth fisherfolk, the volunteer lifesaving station.

Homer had high hopes for this bold although somewhat melodramatic painting, but when he exhibited it in 1883,

Watching the Tempest, 1881

Wreck of the "Iron Crown," 1881

the critics rejected it. He let the picture drop out of sight, and for years it was presumed lost. Ten years later he exhibited another painting, *Gale*, similar to the earlier work, but in fact smaller *(below, right)*. Since then X-ray examination has revealed that both paintings are really one and the same. Homer cut down the original canvas, repainted the sea and added rocks and surf where the lifesaving station, boat and fishermen had been. For his trouble, he was awarded a gold medal, and in 1916, only six years after his death, *Coming Away of the Gale*, alias *Gale*, sold for a record $30,000.

Coming Away of the Gale, 1883,
from a photograph of the painting in its original state

Gale, 1883-1893

Life Line, 1884

Saved, c. 1889

Among the paintings Homer produced soon after he returned from Tynemouth is *Life Line (below)*. On the very first day it was exhibited in New York, a woman collector bought it for $2,500—and so much did Homer welcome this news that he rushed to tell it to his 75-year-old mother. Moreover, the critics accorded the painting the praise that only a year before they had denied *Coming Away of the Gale*. But Homer certainly must have been amused by *The New York Times*'s description of his picture. Noting that the girl being rescued was "by no means ill-favored in figure and face," the reviewer commended the artist for having done "the very unusual thing of uniting cleverness of conception and good composition, with a sensuousness . . . which is none the less admirable because, true as it is, it will not shock the most decorous."

Life Line's popularity—as great as that of *Prisoners from the Front*—prompted Homer to reproduce the picture as an etching *(top, left)*, and again, about five years later, in still another version *(bottom, left)*. In this one, he reversed the figures and enlarged them, simplifying the background, and adding rocks to the upper left corner. But instead of naming the second etching after the well-known *Life Line*, he issued it under the new and anticlimactic title *Saved*.

Study for *Life Line*, 1882-1883

Life Line, 1884

Fog Warning, 1885

Herring Net, 1885

Despite the success of *Life Line* and the new luster it gave his reputation, Homer withdrew from the art world. His brother Charlie had bought land and a large house at Prouts Neck, Maine, with an eye to settling their elderly parents there and perhaps even developing the area as a summer resort, and Homer packed his things and joined the family. He found much to his liking: the sea as he had known it at Tynemouth—even a fishing fleet to provide him with subjects for paintings like these. But his mother was to spend only one season in her grand new house; she died the following spring in New York, and 10 days after her death Winslow returned to the Neck alone. "I went into the house . . . today," he wrote to his sister-in-law Mattie. "Found it in good order. Thought of Mother with a certain amount of pleasure, thank the Lord. I knew that if possible she was with me. I feel quite well for the first time in two weeks."

The effect of Prouts Neck on Homer was salutary: soon he was painting with renewed intensity, and increasing subtlety, as the delicate coloring and scintillating highlights of *Herring Net (above)* show. Gone was any tendency toward overstatement: the fisherman anxiously watching a fog bank close in on his ship in *Fog Warning (opposite)* is as starkly effective a figure as Homer had yet achieved.

109

The mastery toward which Homer was ever striving led him more and more to concentrate on essentials. *The Wreck*, painted 11 years after *Fog Warning*, demonstrates how far he had progressed toward his goal. Using broad, fluid brush strokes and boldly restricting his palette to a few colors, he juxtaposed darks and lights to gain dramatic contrasts. But certainly the most startling

aspect of this monumental painting is the way Homer chose to tell his story. Rather than show the wreck, he concentrated on the rescue operation—even painting out the masts of the ship which he had at first included. The determined rescuers and tense onlookers, standing in small groups like a Greek chorus atop the dunes, powerfully suggest the drama that is being enacted on the other side.

The Wreck, 1896

Kissing the Moon, painted in 1904,
six years before Homer's death, is the
fulfillment in large measure of the simplifying
process seen in *The Wreck*. It is commanding
in its slashing brushwork, strong in color,
bold—even paradoxical—in conception.
All the lifelong independence of Homer
is here, spelled out in daring terms.
Who but he—after careful observation of the
sea at Prouts Neck—would have depicted
his subjects quite this way, with only their
heads and shoulders showing as the boat
they are riding in disappears in the trough
of a wave? The effect is mysterious, still.
In fact, the silence pervading the painting
seems to pull it over from reality into
the realm of a dream. The men sit ramrod
straight as the waves lift in peaks all around
them; the moon shines, but it is the light
of the setting sun that gives their heads their
ruddy glow. The motion—almost a kind of
slow motion—is that of the paint itself,
building strokes of blue into rippling waves.

Kissing the Moon, 1904

VI

Epics of
the Ocean

The paintings that Winslow Homer brought back to America after his two years at Tynemouth in England pleased the post-Civil War critics and connoisseurs because they were more contrived, more "artistic," than Homer's previous work. Receding from direct naturalism, Homer had arranged his subjects in studiedly harmonious compositions which, by their very artificiality, satisfied the New Taste.

However, Homer was not primarily concerned with the praise of professional tastemakers or of connoisseurs who thought they added charm to watercolors by calling them "aquarelles." He envisioned as an ideal showplace for his work not a hushed gallery frequented by rare and refined souls, but a store window in front of which the average man could stop and admire. But even the thought of appealing once more to a wide audience could not deflect Homer for long from his artistic purposes. He would not tailor his work to please either the esthetes or the crowd. He could only paint the best way he knew how and hope that somehow the world would come to understand what he was aiming at.

One result of this uncompromising honesty was that Homer almost immediately moved beyond his popular Tynemouth manner. Only one of the seven major oils he completed in the four years after his return to America shows distinct traces of his English work. This painting is *Undertow*, which pictures two muscular lifeguards and two women whom they have saved from being washed out to sea. The four bodily forms stand out boldly in three dimensions. Homer's biographer Lloyd Goodrich, who considers *Undertow* "one of the strongest figure pieces in modern art," expresses amazement that Homer, who is not known to have ever drawn from the nude, achieved such "full modelling" and "large nobility." The Tynemouth manner is most visible in the way the figures are arranged. Striving to get the same sort of rhythmic effect he had achieved in such Tynemouth paintings as *Hark! the Lark (page 103)*, Homer posed his figures in a way that seems not natural but contrived. The critics, as could be foreseen, were enthusiastic. "Were Mr. Homer a younger man," one wrote, "and thoroughly trained in his art . . . a wonderful future might be predicted for him."

European-trained, William Merritt Chase, leader of the Younger Men, painted brilliant canvases like this still life. Rendered with facile strokes of the brush, the moist fish, gleaming bucket and polished table reveal Chase's emphasis on color and texture.

William Merritt Chase:
Still Life with Fish, c. 1903

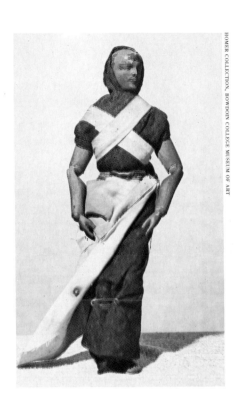

Like most painters, Homer occasionally resorted to the use of mannikins when he wanted to study the play of light on a form, or to try out a pose. This mannikin, found in Homer's studio after his death, still wears the clothes the artist put on it—with a shawl crossed over its chest in the manner of the fisherwomen of Tynemouth.

In the other oil paintings of the post-Tynemouth period, all that Homer had taught himself in England about composition is completely assimilated into his naturalism. The viewer feels no sense of artistic arrangement but rather that this is exactly what the scene must have looked like. The cast of characters is kept small, usually one or two figures, the forms being larger and more monumental than those in Homer's earlier work. Now seeking not charm, not lyricism, not grace, but power, Homer labored to remove everything extraneous, to concentrate on the essential elements that would transmit a stark and compelling message. Children are banished from these new canvases. Women are not decorative or desirable but are shown as representatives of an embattled humanity that must use all its strength to survive. This new and profound view of the human condition is eloquently expressed in an 1884 oil painting called *Life Line (page 107)*.

Homer spent part of the summer after his return from Tynemouth in Atlantic City, New Jersey. There the sailors who manned a very up-to-date lifesaving station got used to the presence of an inquisitive man, dapper and small, who nonetheless had a workman's hands and a practical brain. This strange visitor conversed amiably with the sailors, asking endless questions about a fascinating device the lifesaving station had recently acquired. This was a cannon that could shoot a rope to a wrecked ship offshore. Once the rope was made fast to the distressed vessel, a winch on shore would pull it taut. Along the rope moved a pulley from which a life preserver was hung in a horizontal position, like a seat. On the seat a person from the wreck could be pulled ashore. Homer made numerous sketches of this ingenious contraption.

Soon, according to one story, the roof of the Tenth Street Studios, where Homer had moved to in 1872, bore two living models: a burly mulatto man who sat on a propped-up life preserver, and his sister, who assumed a languid pose on his knees. Supposedly, the painter drenched his models with pails of water. When their forms were wet enough and the light struck them just as he wished, he would begin to paint.

In the finished work the models who had posed safely on Homer's roof, are shown perilously suspended in mid-air. The city has vanished, to be replaced by the aspect of nature that most defies humanity: storm-tossed water. To the left, there is dimly visible a torn rag of sail to indicate the wreck from which the man and woman have come; to the right, there is a more substantial loom of land, their haven; and in the left background, there is a solid stretch of murderous reef. Waves gesture with huge menace at the two figures. To concentrate attention on the woman's face, Homer hid the man's with the wind-whipped end of her scarf. She has fainted, her body limp in her rescuer's strong grasp, her noble and sensitive features composed in helplessness.

The major themes of humanity are universal and thus, if superficially handled, banal: it takes a great artist to see them afresh in their profound significance. A gloss of prettiness, a little less energy, a weakening in sincerity, and *Life Line*, instead of striking with power and moving with eloquence, would seem sentimental. But Homer suffused the painting with conviction and energy; it stands as one of his more impressive works. It certainly escapes the sentimentality that Homer despised. Some years later when a dealer was having trouble selling another of his compositions because it was too stark, Homer wrote sardonically, "If you want more sentiment put into this picture I can with one or two touches, in five minutes time, give it the stomach ache that will suit any customer."

A year after his return from England, in 1883, Homer moved out of the Tenth Street Studios where he had worked for the better part of 11 years and established himself in Prouts Neck, Maine, the fishing village where his family had acquired a summer home. There was a stable near the main house; moving it some 40 yards away, Homer fitted it up as a combined studio and dwelling. Here he was to live, except when he was away on trips, for the remaining 27 years of his life.

Again, as at Tynemouth, Homer was within sight and sound of the sea and his neighbors were members of that stoical breed who make their living upon it. This time, however, they were not Englishmen but state-of-Mainers—blood of his American blood, bone of his Yankee bone. Homer got to know a number of these tough, angular men and evidently persuaded some of them who manned one of the larger boats to take him along on a voyage to the Grand Banks. Back at Prouts Neck he painted, from sketches made on the voyage and from neighbors who obligingly posed for him, a series of oils which are among his greatest works. (He actually finished *Life Line* at Prouts Neck, using a local man, Henry Lee, as a model.)

Herring Net (page 109) could easily be a gay celebration of a successful catch, but Homer emphasized instead the heavy although not unpleasant weariness that accompanies the closing of a day's hard labor. The two figures in their wet oilskins are not shown in the round like the figures in *Undertow;* following the practice that extended back to the woodblocks of his youth, Homer made them suggestive shapes. But how powerful now, how massive in their lack of elaboration! The sky is dark tan; off in the misty twilight one dimly sees a schooner. Yet there is a touch of bright color, of visual gaiety: the little fish in the net are iridescent, painted with quick, light strokes reminiscent of the freedom of Homer's watercolors.

Another oil of the same period, *Lost on the Grand Banks*, which shows two frightened sailors peering over the gunwales of a small boat, is not as successful. The emotions of the protagonists are particularized to the point of pettiness and all of the forms are small and overinsistent. *Fog Warning (pages 108-109)*, however, deals with the same theme heroically and with complete success. The viewer sees a solitary fisherman out in a rowboat on the limitless ocean, staring stoically at the distant schooner where his safety lies but which is about to disappear in an advancing fog. All the main forms are monumental—the boat, the tail of a large fish protruding from its stern, the waves, the human figure— yet nothing is static: one must look twice to realize that the painted boat does not rock and that the oars are motionless. The bearded man dressed in oilskins is generalized, his features no more than broadly indicated, yet the alert pose of the body, the tense hands on the oars, communicate the realization of danger and the marshaling of strength to overcome it.

Eight Bells (detail, slipcase) is, by contrast, laid on a large ship. Two oilskin-clad men are on deck ascertaining bearings with octants: one is shooting the sun; the other, who has just finished doing so, is taking a reading. Here humanity is in control, but the mystery and the wonder of nature surrounds the scene. The sun, glowing from behind clouds, illuminates the vastness of the ocean. The viewer feels that a storm is just ending and that this is perhaps the first time in days that the sailors have been able to take their bearings. But there is no melodrama: the two men are calmly intent on their accustomed mariner's task. The painting's title, which simply refers to the way a ship's bell marks the hours, emphasizes the routine nature of the occasion. The painting is, however, charged with emotion that Homer has provided in some fashion not immediately ascertainable.

When exhibited in New York, Homer's sea epics troubled some of the critics. They carped at his "handling" and the harshness of the colors, so far removed from the felicities of the Younger Men. Still, the impact of the pictures could not be denied. Nor could the impression that a great artist was developing, however peculiarly, at Prouts Neck. Yet collectors hesitated to take the plunge. Only two of Homer's seven sea epics sold, and one of those at a ridiculously low price.

Meanwhile, Homer's exploratory medium, watercolor, once again began to run far ahead of his oil practice, especially in the use of color. Shortly after his return from Tynemouth, Homer executed in watercolor from the Prouts Neck cliffs several pure seascapes, trying to capture the hues, so much brighter than the North Sea grayness, given the water by the shining down-East sun. Although he succeeded to some extent in scaling his palette upward, he was dissatisfied and abandoned for some years his efforts to depict for their own sake the waters off Maine. Instead, he made a pilgrimage to a region where color ran riot.

During December 1884, Homer sailed for the Bahamas. He was in a holiday mood—his mail lay at Prouts Neck unforwarded—and his esthetic objective was simply to hold up a mirror to bright nature. Beneath the warm West Indian sun, all the troubles of the world fell from him. The youthful hedonism that had been so long snowed under was still part of the middle-aged man's temperament, and now it thawed out. He temporarily forgot his maturer emotions. The darker, the more penetrating, could wait until he translated what he now did with such verve into the thoughtful medium of oil.

Again, as at Tynemouth, Homer had no deep contact with the world he painted; but now he was seeking not significance but visual pleasure. If he did not wholly understand the thoughts of the half-naked shark fishermen, of the brown girls carrying bananas on their heads, that made it easier for him to see them purely as shape and color in a brilliant landscape. The bright tropical sun helped him find in nature a new luminousness. Although his pictures did not climb to the highest hues, everything glowed with light, even the rain.

A strange thing was happening to Winslow Homer. The man whose concern with technique had never gone beyond simply trying to find a suitable method to express what he had to say, who throughout his career as a painter in oil had adhered to the simplest and most conservative expedients, was becoming in watercolor a major technical innovator. "Homer," writes the art historian Virgil Barker, "re-made the craft. . . . He invented the handling where everything depends on a trained spontaneity. . . . No one since has added to its technical resources, and it is even unlikely that anyone can."

For centuries the long and glorious history of watercolor had been primarily centered in China and Japan, in Persia and India. In Europe, the medium had been used extensively by medieval manuscript illuminators, but then it had long languished. A revival came in England at the end of the 18th Century. Like so much else that influenced Homer, this resurgence was a response to the new demands of an arising, prosperous and growing middle class.

In England, and by extension in America, watercolor painting was at first largely the preserve of amateurs and popular illustrators. Most of the amateurs were the daughters of prosperous bourgeois families. As more and more such girls received polite educations, art instruction became widespread and the teachers generally taught the use of watercolors—the paper and dry pigments were easier to carry than a canvas and a box of oil paints and the light tints were less likely to soil dresses. Homer's early introduction to the medium grew, of course, from its use in female education: he saw, admired and imitated his mother's colorful renditions of flowers.

Illustrators had begun to use watercolors in response to a wide demand for colored engravings which the unassisted printing press, being limited to black and white, could not supply. The method evolved was to use the press as far as it would go, and then cover the inked forms with transparent watercolor that allowed the shading of the printed image to show through. This was the method used in the popular prints by Currier and Ives. The practice soon became an effective art form. Among the men who used it to produce works of major esthetic importance were the English printer-poet and mystic William Blake, and the American ornithologist-explorer-artist John James Audubon.

As English taste turned increasingly to landscape art, painters took their watercolors out in the fields, first with an eye to the printer and then to create pictures to be displayed in their own right. At the end of a considerable period of development came the work of the English genius Joseph Turner, who was an old man when Homer was a boy, and who was surely the greatest watercolorist before Homer.

Some of Turner's quick nature sketches are as free as Homer's mature watercolors, but these were usually intended as mere notes. When Turner made a watercolor for framing he sought to achieve in the quicker and lighter medium effects parallel to those he achieved in his oil paintings. The pigment was laid on in a static manner, the compositions were formally balanced and the landscape view was likely to be panoramic even if the scale was small. Turner made limited use of the transparency of his washes and would no more have allowed white paper to

A page from Homer's daybook for 1902 lists 10 watercolors the artist had sent to a New York dealer "to net me $200 each . . . good or bad large or small." Number five, complete with sketch, is *Turtle Pound*, the masterpiece reproduced on page 132. When urged by his brother Arthur to make a complete list of his works, Homer replied, "During my lifetime I will know where they are, and after I am dead I won't care."

show in a finished watercolor than he would have allowed bare canvas to show in a finished oil. The watercolorists who followed Turner did not seek spontaneity but used their mounting technical skill to go even further than he had gone in seeking effects that paralleled oil painting.

When Homer first took up watercolor, he started far back in the practice of the art. In the manner of the illustrators, he made detailed drawings and then colored them with washes. But, characteristically, he soon began to go his own way, experimenting to find the best methods offered by the peculiarities of the watercolor medium. He did not, like most of his contemporaries, try to torture the medium into imitating oil paints. Instead he developed the use of watercolors for their own sake, probing for new and different ways in which the light, brilliant tints could be used to capture various subjects. Increasingly he used the white paper's ability to reflect light back through transparent washes of color. In this fashion he made his colors more luminous, putting on the least pigment where he wished the greatest brightness. And Homer found he could paint without first making a careful drawing. Instead he would merely sketch the larger outlines of what he wished to depict and create the rest of his efforts with brush in hand.

Like the French Impressionists, Homer was fascinated by the challenge of capturing an instantaneous view of nature. Since the Impressionists made little use of watercolor, it remained for Homer to develop the medium's potential for rendering the impression of a moment's glance, and this he did with genius. Furthermore, as he drew with his brushes in that rapid rhythm which is natural to the American temperament, often picturing a world of physical activity and stress, he made a discovery which pointed far ahead in the history of art.

Today, artists are concerned not only with controlling *what* the viewer's eye sees, but also *how* the eye sees it, with the activity of the ocular muscles and nerves. A painting that, with line and color, sets up visual kinesthetic tensions will seem more vivid than a painting that does not similarly excite the eye. In his swiftly and boldly painted watercolors, Homer developed the ability to set up these pleasurable tensions and excitements. His paintings seem so alive that they make even Turner's watercolors look static.

Of course, the average viewer, untutored in the physiology and psychology of vision, is unaware of these sources of the enjoyment he feels when looking at a Homer watercolor. And Homer himself, while perhaps instinctively aware of what he was doing, did not think the matter out in theoretical terms. He was simply trying to paint what he saw as exactly, as forcefully and as handsomely as possible. But the result is naturalism carried far beyond its normal limits.

As his ability with watercolor developed, Homer came to view the products not primarily as money-makers or as experiments through which he might improve his oil painting, but rather as important parts of his life work. He even had moments when he believed his fame as a painter would rest on them. "In the future," he told one of his New York dealers, Charles Henschel, "I will live by my watercolors."

It is well that he did not count on his mature watercolors for money.

The innovations that Homer began developing in the 1880s only served to disappoint the critics who had admired the aquarelles he had brought back from Tynemouth. They wanted watercolors that looked like correct oil paintings—carefully composed and with all the white paper covered —and not such apparently careless and even barbaric daubs as these. As the pictures became better and better—and less and less like the work of other men—they ceased to sell with any regularity.

Homer complained bitterly to his agent of the lack of sales. However, he would add in almost the same breath, "I have money in plenty." His family, doing well in Prouts Neck real estate, cut him in on the profits, putting any fear of want behind him. His desire to sell grew from an emotional need to be at one with his environment. While the Younger Men professed scorn of the business society around them, Homer called art his "business" and resented deeply that he made less money, as he said in one letter, than a clerk in a department store.

Looking backward from the 20th Century, conscious of how gloriously his career was to end, one can distinguish in Homer's situation no reason to be discouraged, but discouraged he became. In the three years from 1887 to 1889, he completed no oils, and his watercolor production went down. Instead of painting, he employed much of his energy in trying to win back his youthful popularity by once more making use of the possibilities of the printing press.

He re-did 15 of his Civil War sketches for publication in the *Century Magazine* and subsequently in the four-volume *Battles and Leaders of the Civil War*. And he taught himself an up-to-date reproduction process— etching—that would enable him to make versions of his paintings cheap enough for the public to buy.

The old art of etching was, under the leadership of James McNeill Whistler, being revived by the Younger Men because it presented great possibilities for achieving both brilliance of handling and delicacy of effect. Homer decided to use the medium for his own ends. Taking lessons from a professional etcher, he learned how to cover metal plates with acid-resistant resin and how to scrape this "ground" away with a needle where he wished the acid to bite, thus incising a line in the metal that would hold the ink that was to be transferred to paper. Becoming increasingly expert in the medium as he went along, Homer made versions of some half dozen of his oils and watercolors, including *Life Line*. Although offered at moderate prices—$15 to $30—these etchings did not sell. Connoisseurs did not wish to disturb the refinement of their portfolios with strong, direct renditions of strong, direct paintings; and the general public, if it wanted Homer reproductions at all, was better pleased with photographs of the actual canvases it admired.

In black discouragement, Homer laid aside forever the skill he had achieved as an etcher. His quest for popularity had, so it seemed, made him waste what he called "two years time & hard work." However, for a great artist nothing is altogether wasted. While translating his pictures to copper, Homer had further tightened his already stark compositions, pointing a way to the greatest of his achievements, which he was to produce in the last 20 years of his long, productive life.

Homer's concentration at Prouts Neck was interrupted in 1885 by a visit from his two young nephews, Arthur and Charles—his brother Arthur's boys. He caricatured little Arthur *(above)*, "in fear of harming a worm," and the younger but more rambunctious Charles *(below)*, engaged in his "innocent amusements"—sitting on the cat, pulling the tail of Homer's dog and throwing stones through the studio window.

A Master of Watercolor

Homer was never more relaxed, nor more completely himself, than in his watercolors. They are fresh, spontaneous, alive. Yet they did not come easily: they are the fruit of a long, slow maturation process that can be traced back to his childhood. It was not until the 1870s that he began to paint watercolors with anything approaching the devotion of his later years, and not until the next decade that he gained control over this difficult medium. But in spite of all his hard-won technical excellence, Homer generally restricted his watercolor production to vacation periods. He gave many summers to their creation, finding his subjects on fishing trips in the Adirondacks and the Canadian wilderness. And during the winter he occasionally slipped away to the tropics, with his paintbox packed in his bags.

What makes Homer's watercolors so outstanding is not their subject matter—woods, lakes, rivers, hunters and fishermen, tropical waters and Negroes—but their simplicity and freedom, their transparency and luminosity, their extraordinary color sense, their celebration of physical sensations. They have the feel of weather—the cool press of air in an Adirondack forest, the finger-stiffening chill of a damp Canadian day (*opposite*), the hot edge of a Bahama noon. They distill nature, and while they often include the savage cruelty of the outdoors, they remain consistently beautiful.

Man in nature, the theme of many of Homer's watercolors, comes through strongly in *Osprey's Nest*. Beaching their canoe at the foot of a dead tree, two hunters turn to watch a pair of fish hawks spiral against the dark Canadian sky.

Osprey's Nest, 1902

122

Guide Carrying Deer, 1891

An October Day, 1889

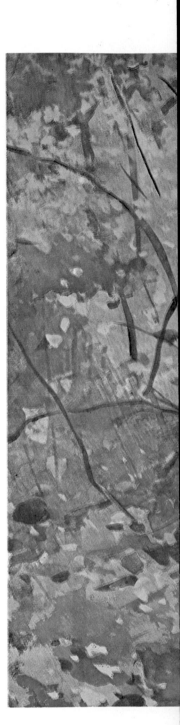

On the Trail, c. 1892

Experimenting with the watercolor medium, Homer soon learned that a quick impression, captured at once on paper, carried more truth than the most carefully worked out detail. *On the Trail (above)* is done with the greatest simplicity: green and brown washes suggest foliage, dabs of color indicate leaves, the narrow track of a pointed brushtip—branches. Almost by sleight of hand, the artist has produced a picture of a forest—and not just any forest, but the Adirondack woods on a gray fall day. His ability, however, never tempted him into being merely facile. *Guide Carrying Deer (top, left)* is carefully composed, structured powerfully on diagonals. *An October Day (bottom, left)*, limpid with color, conceals its strong technique: the wake of the deer in the water is the scraped surface of the paper; the mist hovering on the mountainside is soaked paper and blotted paint.

As he increased his control over the watercolor medium, Homer was able to convey, through the most economical means possible, the spirit of the living moment. This is his achievement in *Shooting the Rapids*, a Canadian scene painted when he was 66. Here, the vigor of his brush conveys the fury of

Shooting the Rapids, 1902

the water; white paper breaking through thin washes catches the reflected
light of an overcast sky; a bleeding area of watery paint in the background
conjures the dense foliage of a hillside. And throughout, muted color captures
the dullness and coolness of the day—black, brown, dark blues and greens.

127

Deer Drinking, 1892

Mink Pond, 1891

On his trips into the wilderness, Homer had a chance to observe —and to paint—nature close up. *A Good Pool (left)* combines all the rushing movement and excitement of *Shooting the Rapids* with an explicitness that makes it possible to identify the hooked, leaping fish as an ouananiche salmon, a landlocked species dwelling in Canada's Saguenay River. The faintest of pencil lines, visible under the thin paint, were all that Homer needed to guide this flashing image from his mind's eye onto paper.

Deer Drinking (above, left) captures a rare instant: a wild animal caught in an unexpected pose. The spontaneity of this watercolor is deceptive; seemingly done on the spot, the picture could really have been painted only from memory, long after the deer, alerted by the artist's presence, had leaped away.

The intimate nature study *Mink Pond (above)* reveals another facet of Homer's genius for watercolor: a delicacy, a finesse, a gentle sensitivity rare in his work. In its style and in its composition, the painting exudes an oriental air.

A Good Pool, Saguenay River, 1895

Of the many watercolors Homer produced from the 1880s onward, the most brilliant are those he painted in the tropics. The sun shines in them with a shimmering brightness new to his work, as though its southern warmth had melted the aging artist's Yankee reserve. Colors appear which were denied him in the north woods—fresh greens, reds, bright blues—and often a figure will again be prominent in the foreground, as in *Under the Coco Palm* (*below*). The sensitivity to weather that Homer showed in his northern watercolors is also evident in his southern pictures: there is humidity, as well as heat, in *Palm Trees, Florida* (*opposite*), a graceful study of tropical vegetation, with fronds pinwheeling like fireworks against the sky.

Homer's watercolors of the tropics captivated the critics and public alike, and they sold well, but at prices that by today's standards seem trifling—$200, $300. The artist gave *Under the Coco Palm* to a Prouts Neck contractor in partial payment for some construction work. When the recipient sold the picture in 1920, it brought enough to put his son through medical school.

Under the Coco Palm, 1898

Palm Trees, Florida, c. 1904

131

One of the qualities that distinguish Homer's watercolors is their sense of design. *Sloop, Bermuda (right)* impresses not by its color alone but by its harmonies. Rhythms lace through the picture—the loops of sail, the clean lines of the boat repeated in the dinghy behind it, the undulating swells of water, the churned turbulence of the sky.

Another quality setting Homer's watercolors apart is their ability to suggest, through mere flicks of the brush, the bodies and features of men. The Negroes below were not intended by the artist to be character studies. Yet because of the skill with which he painted them, they are not just types but carry the weight of real men. Homer's accomplishment here is the more remarkable because it looks so completely effortless. Actually it took all the skill and control at his command to build up the faces and their highlights with washes of color and still preserve a transparency. It was a performance like this that led Homer to say, "You will see, in the future I will live by my watercolors."

Turtle Pound, 1898

Sloop, Bermuda, 1899

VII

Two Fellow Giants

In his portrait of the physicist
Henry A. Rowland, Thomas
Eakins reveals why he is
considered, along with Homer,
one of the greatest representatives
of the naturalistic movement in
America. His meticulousness
extended even to the frame,
which he constructed and carved
with the signs and symbols
of Rowland's profession.

Thomas Eakins:
Professor Henry A. Rowland, 1891

Modern criticism is almost unanimous in linking Winslow Homer, Thomas Eakins and Albert Pinkham Ryder as the three leading American painters of the latter part of the 19th Century. Although very different in many ways, they had in common, in addition to superior quality, several basic characteristics that separated them from the Europeanized Younger Men who were then receiving the most critical acclaim. Like Homer, Eakins and Ryder turned their backs on the doctrine of Art for Art's Sake. They were totally unconcerned with what was up to date or fashionable or correct according to accepted European canons. Instead, they concentrated on expressing their own feelings and experiences as powerfully as they could.

Eakins' distance from the prevailing fashions is the more significant because, far from being self-taught like Homer and Ryder, he had sought an elaborate schooling in art, including study in Paris. A masterly technician, he could have painted in any style that pleased the current taste. But he chose not to follow any of them, remaining as stiffly independent as any painter who ever lived.

Ryder was also independent, but in a wholly different way. Although largely self-taught and completely home-grown, he did not, like Homer and the Hudson River School, depict the scenery or the people of his native land. Instead, he painted dreams, visions and scenes from mythology or the Bible. But even in his renditions of Biblical material he discarded every accepted formula of art, recording instead what glowed on the secret screen of his own unique imagination. In contrast to Homer and Eakins, both such down-to-earth realists, Ryder was the epitome of the mystical artist.

No soil is receptive to every kind of seed; in mid-19th Century America such otherworldly minds as Ryder had not been encouraged to paint. The strong current sweeping the nation's art toward realism and away from fantasy is seen in the contrast between the career of Thomas Cole and the development of the Hudson River School that he set in motion. Cole himself painted in two styles—one, the "ideal," in which he heightened his landscapes with Roman ruins or other historical or imaginative details, and a second which was a direct celebration of the beauties of the American landscape. His successors were either completely unconcerned with, or scornful of, the "ideal" side of his work. They became pure landscapists, thus contributing to that deep current of naturalism that swept into the work of Winslow Homer. There was a similar development in genre: John Quidor's imaginative style gave way to the realism of William Sidney Mount—again presaging the course of Homer's career.

But purely imaginative painting did not altogether vanish: it sank into that substratum of artistic creation that some critics call folk art. Although most simple artists pursued, however haltingly, the reigning realism, some young ladies restive in the strait jacket of polite finishing-school education, some house painters asmolder with a divine fire beyond their ability to kindle or express, occasional eccentrics residing in dark alleys—these painted their own visions, romantic or hallucinatory, sober or alcoholic. Before the advent of Ryder, this obscure churning had turned up only one significant artist, William Rimmer.

Rimmer's father was among the not-inconsiderable group of mid-century Americans who believed that the Dauphin—the eldest son of Louis XVI and youthful heir to the French throne—had not died during the French Revolution, as the world had been told. On the contrary, each of these Americans was convinced that he himself was that Dauphin, and therefore the rightful King of France. Rimmer was raised in a Boston slum by his self-styled royal father who told him they were in hiding lest assassins hired by the "usurper," Louis XVIII, slit their throats. The child's body was half-starved, but his imagination was overstimulated.

After he had grown up and his father had died of alcoholism, Rimmer attempted many professions, including those of self-taught sculptor and painter. In sad and angry isolation, he taught himself both arts so imperfectly—except for his excellent draftsmanship—that the authentic genius he possessed was most severely shackled. His sculpture is so close to greatness that its failure is harrowing. Of his many paintings only one is truly strong: weird, moving, uninterpretable in any reasonable terms, *Flight and Pursuit*, which shows a toga-clad figure running in terror on some violent mission beside his spectral double, commemorates like a shining gravestone a buried career.

Ryder's childhood was not dazzled by any imperial pretensions. His father remained frankly what he was, a dealer in fuel and a customhouse officer at the port of New Bedford, Massachusetts. Yet there was romance enough to enchant the little boy's heart, for New Bedford was the world center of the glamorous whaling trade. The sea came earlier and more naturally to Ryder than to Homer. Two of his brothers went on voyages as sailors, and among Ryder's early memories was how one of these lads had been so pleased to get home after months at sea that he kissed the family's pig.

Homer was drawn to the ocean from New York City by temperamental need. Ryder moved to New York at the age of 21 when his father changed jobs—but he carried with him a vision of the ocean. Long be-

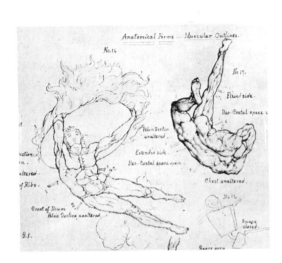

William Rimmer, sculptor, painter and art instructor, was considered by his contemporaries to know the human body better than any other artist. He drew upon this knowledge in his *Art Anatomy*, a book with more than 700 drawings, some of which showed figures falling. Rimmer emphasized emotion and character as much as he did structure. "Make your men deep-chested and narrow-waisted, like a lion," he told his students, "for we live in this world not by let but by opposition."

fore this he had been largely cut off from clear sight of the real world. While he was still a boy his eyes had been so weakened—his parents believed the cause was a misapplied vaccination—that he had been unable to carry his studies beyond elementary school. Perhaps it was this very weakness that turned his attention inward to the fantastic scenes that became his paintings.

In his later years, Ryder wrote a magazine article which summarized his early artistic development in a kind of parable. He had first tried to imitate the great masters. Finding this a "futile struggle," as he put it, "I went out into the fields, determined to serve nature as faithfully as I had served art. In my desire to be accurate I became lost in a maze of detail." Then one day he saw "the old scene . . . framed in an opening between two trees," stand out "like a painted canvas. . . . There was no detail to vex the eye. Three solid masses of form and color— the sky, foliage, and earth—the whole bathed in an atmosphere of golden luminosity," confronted him. "I threw my brushes aside; they were too small for the work in hand. I squeezed out big chunks of pure moist color and taking my palette knife, I laid on blue, green, white and brown in great sweeping strokes. . . . I saw nature springing into life upon my dead canvas. It was better than nature, for it was vibrating with the thrill of a new creation. Exultantly I painted until the sun sank below the horizon, then I raced around the fields like a colt let loose, and literally bellowed for joy."

The bits of professional instruction Ryder accepted in New York City had no appreciable effect on his work. His technique, indeed, remained almost tragically faulty. Whereas most untrained artists at least used permanent sign painter's colors, Ryder's passionate urge for self-expression made him employ whatever best enabled him to externalize his vision at the instant. To a friend who expressed horror at finding him painting with candle grease, Ryder replied defensively that he had used only one small candle. Further argument over his methods would elicit from him the statement that only beauty mattered. If a composition had beauty, that would remain, however much the picture deteriorated physically. This has proved true to some degree—Ryder's pictures are still moving—but old photographs reveal that they were often much more beautiful when they left his easel.

Ryder was in his mid-twenties when he found his first style: small, squarish landscapes in which effectively delineated cattle and horses glimmer in a strange light—half-gloaming, half-dream. Some 10 years later he leaped into a visionary world resembling the one long cultivated by folk artists across the nation, who depicted the great legends of mankind quite naturally, without any display of learning, as if they had invented the legends for themselves. Faraway and vanished places, the great dreams of mankind—these remained close to the imaginations of simple people. Such wonders throbbed in their own skies like the northern lights.

The smallest suggestion could spur Ryder's imagination. A bit of moonlight glowing on a city street could evoke the vastness of the ocean, or a camel gleaming before an Arab's tent, or the white skull of

When in his thirties he painted this self-portrait, Albert Pinkham Ryder seemed already to be looking inward. As his introspection increased, he turned to poetry as another way of expressing himself. Here are two stanzas of "The Voice of the Night," which match the mood of his paintings:

The wind, the wind, the wind
That am I, that am I
My unseen wanderings
Who can pursue, who comprehend?
Soft as a panther treads
When moving for its prey
I fly over beds of sweet roses
And violets pale,
Till disturbed within their slumbers
They bend from my gay caress,
Only to lift their heads again
And send the aroma of sweet perfumes
To call me yet again
Ere I pass away.
. . . . .

But I am the wind, the wind, the wind
I'll away to gloomy pools profound
And stir the silence
Of their reflective depths
With rippling laughter
At my wanton freaks.
And my fantastic wanderings
Who can pursue, who comprehend?

a skeleton riding a ghostly horse around a deserted race track. Increasingly, indeed, his dreams overwhelmed reality, until he saw nothing except what he wanted to see. Remaining unmarried, he became an urban recluse who piled his rooms to the ceiling with broken furniture and old cereal boxes, leaving only narrow paths to his bed, stove and easel. He would never allow the landlord to make repairs, so that the plaster fell and the wallpaper dangled. He could not remember to wash. A big man with a full reddish beard and gentle, visionary eyes, he gave off, through the ragged clothes that he insisted ventilated his body, "certain odors" which made it difficult for fastidious people to stay in the room with him. However, he was completely unconscious of the squalor in which he lived.

Concerning the pair of rooms he rented in a simple, old-fashioned house on New York's West 15th Street, he wrote, "I have two windows in my workshop that look out upon an old garden whose great trees thrust their green-laden branches over the casement sills, filtering a network of light and shadow on the bare boards of my floor. Beyond the low roof tops of neighboring houses sweeps the eternal firmament with its ever-changing panorama of mystery and beauty. I would not exchange these two windows for a palace with less vision than this old garden with its whispering leafage—nature's tender gift to the least of her little ones. . . . The artist needs but a roof, and a crust of bread and his easel, and all the rest God gives him in abundance. He must live to paint and not paint to live. . . . Upon the potboiler is inscribed the epitaph of his art."

The ocean became for Ryder a symbol of the great imponderables through which man sails the mysterious craft of life. Sometimes on its darkly opalescent surface the shape of a shadowy sailboat harmonizes mystically with the cabalistic signs formed by the clouds above. Or the ocean may bubble as Jonah is about to be swallowed by the whale *(pages 154-155)*. Or some bearded sailors may look up from their small boat to see the legendary Flying Dutchman on his eternal voyage in his tremendous schooner, a ship half-reality, half-mist, whose streaming orange sails merge with the sunset *(pages 152-153)*.

Ryder usually bathed the earth in a half-light which the viewer accepts as real but which is so much of the mind that the artist sometimes did not even know whether he was painting night or day. If the moon hangs in these pictures, that enhances their strangeness, for his canvases burn with dim colors the real moon never saw. In one of the artist's most mysterious works, *Siegfried and the Rhine Maidens*, which Ryder painted while under the influence of Richard Wagner's surging music, a sunset is reinforced by a moon glowing with unnatural brightness. Both illuminate a knight in armor, phosphorescent with some inner incandescence that is linked to the strangeness of his mission, as he stops under a tree to talk to three gesticulating maidens bathing in a salmon-colored river.

Much of Ryder's mature work is close to the sweep of romantic music. Although he was often inspired by literature, he was the least literary painter imaginable. He usually left far behind him the stories he started with, since as soon as the initial forms of a picture were on canvas they established for him an emotional relationship of their own. His method was similar to Inness' in its reliance on free association, but, where Inness moved with electrical speed, Ryder advanced in the slowest motion. His pictures hung around him by the dozens like so many dear friends, or sometimes lay face downward in disgrace in the clutter of his studio. They were, he said, "ripening under the sunlight of the years that come and go." He "pondered over" them with "prayer and fasting." Finally, the day would come when he would touch one with his brush, but the touch would produce the most infinitesimal change of mass and color. For his means were as subtle as the message finally conveyed is elusive and profound.

So completely different from the work of either the Younger Men or of the Native School, Ryder's pictures were accepted for exhibition by both the new Society of American Artists, which had been founded by the Younger Men, and by the older National Academy. His strange evocativeness always attracted some purchasers, and toward the turn of the century he became a rage. Collectors besieged his studio and forgers turned out many spurious Ryders to cash in on the demand, but he still refused to be hurried and rarely allowed a canvas out of his hands. To one importunate collector, he wrote, "Have you ever seen an inch worm crawl up a leaf or twig, and then clinging to the very end, revolve in the air, feeling for something to reach something? That's like me. I am trying to find something out there beyond the place on which I have a footing."

In this, as in most other characteristics, Ryder was the opposite of Thomas Eakins. Eakins had little urge to find the "something out there beyond" and he had trained himself so thoroughly to be a painter that there was nothing he wished to accomplish that he could not do instantly. Where Ryder as a boy had wandered about dreamily, Eakins had built a steam engine that ran. His bent seemed as much for mechanics as for art. It was probably his father's interest in design—he was a Philadelphia writing master and calligrapher—that turned Eakins' ambitions away from science and toward painting.

Shortly after his graduation from a Philadelphia high school in 1861, Eakins entered The Pennsylvania Academy of the Fine Arts. It was the oldest art institution in the country and its dusty curriculum reflected its age. Here Eakins drew in pencil or charcoal month after month, for the most part copying plaster casts of famous antique statues. This course of study he varied in the most extreme way by attending classes in anatomy at Jefferson Medical College, and dissecting cadavers at a hospital, in order to learn how the body is made. Thus he occupied himself for almost five years without presuming to attempt to paint.

Then Paris! There he enrolled under the famous Academician Gérôme and began another long course of study. Although he now worked mostly from the living model and soon with oil paints, his objective remained unchanged: not to make a picture, but to learn to reproduce exactly what was before him. Three more years passed, and then Eakins

The sad state today of many of Ryder's paintings can be attributed to thick layers of paint that failed to dry. A close-up of one of his works reveals how even today drops of fluid welling up through cracks ooze out onto the paint surface. This kind of unstable material moves like lava beneath the crust, escaping its fragile trap wherever it can.

felt that, "sooner than I dared hope," he was able to construct the human figure in paint on canvas.

Students, including Eakins' fellow Americans, commonly welcomed this stage in their education because they were now considered free to embroider over the naturalism they had mastered with felicities of "handling." But Eakins broke with the attitude of the Younger Men by viewing such possibilities with scorn. He mocked the "wonderful studies" made by his classmates "to show off, to catch a medal, to please a professor, or to catch the prize of Rome. . . . There are enough difficulties in painting itself, without multiplying them, without searching what is useless to vanquish."

Thus the student of eight years' standing reverted even while he was studying in a Parisian art academy to the old attitude of the American Native School. He was not concerned with elegance, with brilliance, with skills of expression that called the viewer's attention to the painter, but rather with an image which seemed to be nature reproduced. Nature as it presented itself unedited to the eye inspired in Eakins both reverence and affection. As he wrote his father from Paris, "I love sunlight and children and beautiful women and men, their heads and hands, and most everything I see, and some day I expect to paint them as I see them."

Eakins had still not attempted to paint out-of-doors. To learn how became his next technical objective. He obviously did not take it too seriously, since he combined his attack on this new problem with his first effort at a finished picture. The locale was southern Spain, which he now visited, and the subject a picturesque family of dancing gypsies; the result was confusion, perplexity, frustration and finally a very mixed-up composition.

For Eakins outdoor light was never to be a major concern. Wishing to have everything on his canvases under logical control, he regarded those nuances of light that were enchanting American and French Impressionists as "botherations." Thus the fiasco of his Spanish composition did not inspire him to undertake a course of sketching under the sky. It inspired him to go home.

He had come to the conclusion that was to separate him most completely from the Younger Men. Subject matter was to him of primary importance, and it could not be exotic. He could only paint deeply what he deeply understood. So he hurried back to the unpretentious house in Philadelphia where he had lived since he was two. He was to live in it for the rest of his life, never crossing the ocean again.

Soon after his return to Philadelphia, Eakins began painting the sports that both he and his father enjoyed, particularly rowing on the local Schuylkill River. The effect of these canvases on the eye is one of complete naturalism, but the brain recognizes an agreeable sense of order, such as was to be achieved more conspicuously at a later date in landscapes influenced by Cubism. The sunlight is bright and satisfying, yet the picture contains more of what the mind remembers of a clear day than of what the eye sees. The boats and their occupants are spaced as they might actually appear at a moment when chance had arranged them in a geometrical pattern. The mood is not the gay hedonism of Homer's vacation rhapsodies, but is rather one of sober, rational enjoyment.

Eakins' art was always to remain essentially serious, without smiles, without graces. To its service he brought the mathematics he loved. If one wished to paint a boat in the position of sailing, he expounded, it was necessary to calculate three different angles or tilts: the boat's direction in relation to the picture plane, its reaction to the wind, and its reaction to the waves. "Now the way to draw her," Eakins told one of his art classes, "is to enclose her in a simple brick-shaped form, to give in mechanical drawing the proper tilts, one at a time, to the brick form, and finally to put the tilted brick into perspective and lop off the superabounding parts."

Eakins had been home for four years—he was 31—when he executed an ambitious composition that was a bid, like a French student's Salon picture, for serious recognition. However, the subject was far from all accepted taste in art. In the same hospital where he had studied and dissected, Eakins painted an operation. The attention is not on the unfortunate patient, nor on his mother, who in her pose of horror is pushed off to one side. The composition is expertly managed to cast attention on the surgeon, Dr. Samuel Gross. He stands, a scalpel in his hand, with his back to the patient, whom other doctors attend. He is using the patient's pain and danger to further science by quietly lecturing on what is taking place to students who lounge in the dimly indicated amphitheater. There is blood on the surgeon's hand, but the overall mood is efficient and routine.

Eakins' *Gross Clinic (page 145)* is today considered a masterpiece, but it shocked the people of its own time. One critic wrote, "To sensitive and instinctively artistic natures such a treatment as this one, of such a subject, must be felt as a degradation of Art." The blood on the surgeon's hand was something critics and patrons particularly objected to. This only brought out the artist's pugnacity. When, 14 years later, he painted a similar operating-room scene, the *Agnew Clinic*, he again put blood (this time over the surgeon's own objection) on the protagonist's hand. Again he was called a "butcher," and again his feelings were lacerated by the hostile critics and public.

Eakins' two hospital paintings so feature the surgeon that they are, in essence, portraits of men in action. Interest in portraiture grew on Eakins as the years passed until his output consisted almost exclusively of likenesses, often of people hard at work at their professions.

Since Gilbert Stuart's death in the 1820s, portraiture in the United States had fallen on evil days, becoming less art than efficient craftwork or an exercise in social flattery. The greatest flatterer of them all was Eakins' younger contemporary John Singer Sargent. Born in America but raised abroad in a succession of hotels and rented villas, Sargent had imbibed in France a style sensational for its brilliant technical handling. With a single, seemingly unpremeditated brushstroke, he could communicate form and color and texture—the look and feel of reality. He used this virtuosity to create glittering society images

Thomas Eakins' teacher, the French Academician Jean-Léon Gérôme, produced this smoother-than-life painting of the mythical sculptor Pygmalion embracing his statue of Galatea. Although Eakins greatly admired Gérôme, he did not paint like him and decried the artificial content of much French art—"smiling, smirking goddesses of many complexions, amidst the delicious arsenic green trees and gentle wax flowers and purling streams a-running up and down the hills, especially up."

Painter Thomas Eakins also tried his hand at sculpture. He carved these oval reliefs in clay as chimney pieces; they had been commissioned, and he went to great trouble over them. He even had the model for the relief shown below take spinning lessons and he became so fascinated by her increasing dexterity that he destroyed all that he had finished in order to begin again. But as very often happened to Eakins, his rich client rejected the reliefs before they could be carved in stone.

that made him the darling of the rich on two continents. His pictures are almost the opposite of Eakins' work. Where a Sargent portrait is best at first glance and then slowly deflates under scrutiny, Eakins' portraits may at first seem repellent but become more impressive the longer one looks.

Not satisfied, as Sargent was, with rendering exteriors, Eakins, who had dissected to learn how to paint the bones and sinews of the human body, wished also to get below the surfaces of the human mind. Nor was Eakins interested in Sargent's sitters, those social and business leaders of the Gilded Age. He invited his intellectual friends—professors, scientists, musicians, artists, as well as pupils and neighbors—to sit for him. Usually he offered to give them their portraits; often they went off in deep depression, refusing to take the pictures with them. One of the few paintings he did of businessmen was destroyed by the sitter's family because they did not wish "his descendants to think of their grandfather as resembling such a portrait." For as Eakins' view of the world grew increasingly somber, he explored for the darkness in his sitters, showing them combative and defiant, or shrinking, or exhausted and withdrawn. This was true even when he painted women. He would seek out pretty ones, and then exhume whatever despair or frustration or lassitude lay well hidden under their charms.

Eakins' ability to strike to the truth was perhaps best summed up in one sentence by the poet Walt Whitman, of whom Eakins did in the late 1880s a remarkable portrait *(page 150)*. "I never knew of but one artist, and that's Tom Eakins," Whitman said, "who could resist the temptation to see what they thought ought to be rather than what is."

More than any other American painter, Eakins could paint the figure, clothed or nude, so that it stands before the viewer fully realized on canvas. The heads are breathtakingly like living heads seen in three-dimensional reality. In every picture there is thus a plastic vitality that is in itself exciting. But the final meaning or significance of Eakins' art is less immediately visible. Often Eakins' attitude puts the viewer off, as one is put off by a person who constantly tells other people unpleasant truths about themselves. Only when one ceases to think of Eakins' portraits as social acts, considering them instead as works of art independent of the feelings of the sitters, does the realization come through that these are profound comments on the human condition. Many of the paintings are, indeed, studies in the alienation of intellectual men and women from a hostile world.

However, Eakins always saw, even in those individuals who seem most defeated, a heartening resilience, a biological gallantry that makes it possible for life to go on. Pity resides in Eakins' brush, but it is not the pity of moist eye and reassuring smile. It is the surgeon's pity as he probes the cancer.

Whereas Homer and Ryder withdrew from the Gilded Age into the countryside or into dreams and at last became recluses, Eakins fought what he considered the good fight in the lists of Philadelphia. His worldly activity was that of the Younger Men: teaching future professionals to paint. His battle was against prudery, and against the infiltration of a great calling by a false gentility.

As director of the Pennsylvania Academy, where he himself had begun his formal art studies, he based his instruction on the nude model. However, the trustees of the Academy and their friends had daughters who claimed to have artistic souls and who needed, in any case, to be kept out of mischief until they got married. Young ladies swarmed into the Academy, and when Eakins insisted that if they were to study there they had to "face the absolute nude," he was discharged in a public scandal. Continuing the crusade in other art schools, he lost again and again until, despite the great success he had instructing his men students and the more serious women, he became unemployable as a teacher.

Eakins had been among the first of the foreign-trained American students to return to the United States. That was in 1870, when his naturalistic approach to subject matter appealed to the still dominant Native School taste. He was regarded as a coming man, even if his pictures were only beginning to sell. But then students who had stayed in the foreign schools past the point where he had left brought home their little studies, their brilliancies of handling, and Eakins' serious, heavy, almost brutally realistic renditions of American character made him seem an opponent rather than an advocate of beauty. He was—in his words—"persuaded to join" the Society of American Artists and for a while he exhibited there. However, as more Younger Men flocked in, the Society regularly rejected his work in favor of pictures he considered "frivolous and superficial." In 1892 he angrily resigned.

Fortunately, Eakins had a small private income which prevented the world from tying him down by his pocketbook. He almost never made a sale. During most of his career, he was encouraged only by a small circle of friends and disciples. He was an old man, and the 20th Century had dawned, when a revolt against the dilettantism of the now elderly Younger Men brought him belated celebrity. In 1904 the Pennsylvania Academy, from which he had been discharged, offered him a gold medal. He appeared with a disciple, both in bicycling costume, to pick it up. Commenting that the Academy had "a heap of impudence" to give him a medal, he promptly cycled on to the Philadelphia mint where he derisively turned the gold emblem into cash.

Now the newspapers came to him for interviews and after years of silence suddenly began calling him the "dean of American painters." But when he was asked who was the greatest painter in America, he replied, "Winslow Homer." And he added, "If America is to produce great painters and if young art students wish to assume a place in the history of the art of their country, their first desire should be to remain in America, to peer deeper into the heart of American life. . . . It would be far better for American art students and painters to study their own country and portray its life and types. . . . Of course, it is well to go abroad and see the works of the old masters, but Americans . . . must strike out for themselves, and only by doing this will we create a great and distinctly American art."

Individualists Three

Winslow Homer, Thomas Eakins and Albert Pinkham Ryder could not have been more unlike as individuals. Homer was close-mouthed, down-to-earth, fastidious; Eakins gregarious, intellectual, unkempt; Ryder dreamy, disorganized, dirty. But all three men shared certain basic principles and their greatness stems in large measure from their absolute refusal to compromise and lessen the power of their art.

Eakins, the realist, fought a public that demanded reality in painting—but only the nice kind. The blood he showed on the hands of Dr. Gross in the masterwork reproduced on the opposite page brought him condemnation as a "butcher." Even Ryder would win more critical acclaim with his visions than Eakins with his precise and probing views of life. And whereas Homer would at least have the satisfaction of seeing all but one of the oils he had finished at Prouts Neck over a 26-year period sold before he died, Eakins would leave an entire houseful of pictures behind him upon his death.

In a way, Eakins and Homer complemented each other. Homer approached his subjects pictorially and intuitively, Eakins plastically and logically. The poet Walt Whitman remarked about Eakins that he painted not what ought to be, but what is; the same could be said of Homer. Ryder, on the other hand, although also remaining true to his experience, painted quite another reality—an internal one, that of the mind.

Scalpel in hand, Dr. Samuel Gross turns away from an operation to address his students in one of the most powerful and controversial of Eakins' paintings. Behind the doctor, to the left, is the patient's mother, hiding her eyes from the sight of the incision in her son's thigh.

Thomas Eakins: *Gross Clinic*, 1875

Ignored as a pioneer in the development of motion pictures, Eakins was actually the first American to take multiple exposure photographs of a moving subject—here an athlete jumping—with a single camera. Other contemporary experimenters used a whole battery of cameras.

Eakins: *Swimming Hole*, 1883

A love of sports and the outdoor life, combined with an admiration for the human body, led Eakins on occasion to paint men and women nude. He even included himself naked in *Swimming Hole (below, left)*; he is the swimmer in the right foreground. To Eakins, the nude was "the most beautiful thing there is," but to many of his contemporary Philadelphians, the unclothed body was shameful, certainly not a fit subject for an artist's brushes. Boldly Eakins made anatomy and the study of the nude the basis of his instruction at The Pennsylvania Academy of the Fine Arts. Inevitably this caused a public scandal. When he removed a loincloth from a male model in a women's drawing class to demonstrate the muscles of the groin, he so rocked the community at large that he had no alternative but to resign. Actually, Eakins himself painted relatively few nudes; his early concern with the body shifted to human character as he became increasingly a portraitist. Late in his career, however, Eakins renewed his interest in sports, especially boxing, and in such paintings as *Between Rounds (below)* he once again showed his appreciation of the body as the noble structure it is.

Eakins: *Between Rounds*, 1899

Eakins' advice to his students was to "strain your brain more than your eye." He loved mathematics, and, tense from a day's work, he would often relax by reading logarithmic tables. "In mathematics," he said, "the complicated things are reduced to simple things. So it is in painting." Nothing illustrates this better than his own perspective studies for his oils. At right is a drawing which shows how painstakingly Eakins worked out the spatial relationships of the furniture in a room before placing his subjects in it. Below is another perspective drawing. Traced onto canvas, it became the framework on which Eakins could build *Oarsmen (bottom, right)*—one of several paintings he did of men in sculls.

To the end of his life Eakins remained an artist who constructed his paintings logically. He trusted inspiration, but invariably he analyzed what his eyes saw before assembling it on canvas. His works seem to stop time. It is as though the clock in *Chess Players (far right)* had paused between ticks, making silence—and thought—pervasive.

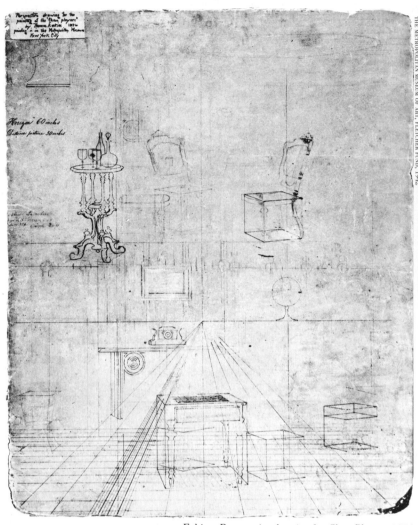

Eakins: Perspective drawing for *Chess Players*, 1876

Eakins: Perspective drawing for *Oarsmen*, c. 1872

Eakins: *Chess Players*, 1876

Eakins: *Oarsmen*, 1872

Eakins: *Walt Whitman*, detail, 1887

Eakins: *Self Portrait*, detail, 1902

Eakins: *Addie*, detail, 1900

Eakins: *A. W. Lee*, detail, 1905

Intellectual though his approach to art may have been, Eakins had his full measure of feeling, too. His portraits, more than any of his other works, make this clear. Whether the subject was himself, his wife, a friend or someone he barely knew, he managed to penetrate to the core of the personality. There is no illusion, no conceit, in his self-portrait *(above)*. Eakins shows himself for what he was—a sad man, well aware of rejection, yet able to bear it. His gift was to catch people at the moment they lapsed into themselves. His response was almost always compassionate, as in the portrait of his childhood friend Mary "Addie" Williams *(center, left)*. His wife *(opposite)*, wilting into her chair, appears defenseless and resigned. Walt Whitman *(top, left)*, on the other hand, presents a ruddy face and a robust temperament to the world—but, for all that, wears lace on the edge of his shirt collar. The poet did not like his portrait at first, but the more he lived with it the deeper he found its insight. "Eakins is not a painter," Whitman said. "He is a force."

Incapable of flattering his subjects, the artist often ended by offending them. In his painting of a Philadelphia businessman, A. W. Lee *(bottom, left)*, there is a deathly coldness. When the time arrived for Lee to take the finished painting home, he politely paid for it—and left it in the artist's studio.

Eakins: *Lady with a Setter Dog*, 1885

151

Albert Pinkham Ryder: *Flying Dutchman*, c. 1887

Ryder: *Marine*, c. 1890

Whereas Eakins and Homer looked outward, finding their inspiration in reality, Albert Pinkham Ryder turned inward and discovered another whole world to paint in his mind. A visionary, he needed little more than "a rain-tight roof . . . a box of colors and God's sunlight" to remain true to his dreams. He painted only 150 or so pictures over a lifetime, all of them small, often spending years on his canvases—allowing them, as he put it, to "ripen." So intense an inner life did Ryder lead that he was oblivious to the disorder and filth of his rooms. "I never see all this," he said, "unless someone comes to see me."

Ryder conceived his paintings in terms of masses and rhythms, and he willfully distorted objects and simplified shapes to project them as symbols of his visions. He is most famous for his moonlit marine paintings, like the one above, a lyric poem in contrast to the sonorous prose of a Homer seascape. Ryder's inspiration came from many sources, including New York Harbor, and at night he used to wander for hours through the city soaking up the moonlight with which he drenched his works. Just as he loved the sea, Ryder was thrilled by music. Wagner's opera *The Flying Dutchman* so inspired him that he rushed home after a performance to record his feelings in paint, creating one of his most dramatic works *(left)*.

Ryder: *Temple of the Mind*, c. 1885

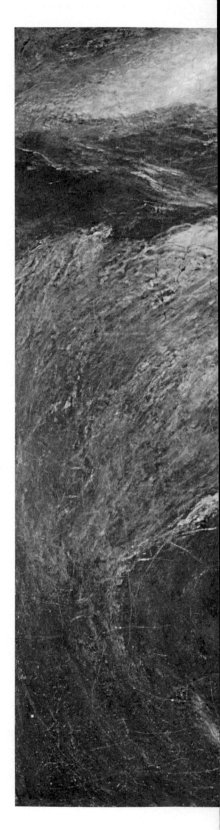

In his efforts to set down his dreams, Ryder often employed unsound methods and, as a result, his canvases have deteriorated, some almost beyond salvation. His *Temple of the Mind (above)* retains a haunting beauty, despite the cracking and discoloration which make it almost impossible to see either the Three Graces or the cloven-hoofed fauns. *Jonah (opposite)* has fared somewhat better: the color is stronger and the boat and its passengers—even Jonah in the water and God in heaven—can be discerned, as can the whale looming at the right. But until recently this was not so—the picture had begun to crack like the drying mud of a swamp. Through the efforts of the conservators Sheldon and Caroline Keck, however, *Jonah* was saved and brought back to something like its original beauty.

"I am in ecstasys over my Jonah," Ryder wrote to a dealer while he was still working on the painting. "Such a lovely turmoil of boiling water and everything. . . . If I get the scheme of color that haunts me: I think you will be delighted." In his complete subjectivity Ryder pointed toward one of the directions American painting would take in the 20th Century. "Modern art must strike out from the old," the artist said. "The new is not revealed to those whose eyes are fastened in worship upon the old."

154

Ryder: *Jonah,* c. 1890

VIII

Loneliness and Triumph

Cannon Rock, the title of this Homer oil, is also the name of a Prouts Neck landmark. In painting the rock, Homer changed its height and profile somewhat for the sake of design, then patiently waited for the right wave to form before finishing the picture.

Cannon Rock, 1895

The companions of Winslow Homer's later years were the companions of his childhood—his father (who did not die until 1898, when Winslow was 62) and his two brothers. With the brothers' wives, all spent their summers at Prouts Neck, where the family was profitably engaged in superimposing a vacation community on the original fishing village. Winslow lived by himself in his studio, but it was only a stone's throw from the family's main house, called the Ark, where he commonly dined if any of his relatives were about. When he went off on fishing trips it was with Charles, the older brother who had always been his best friend. And even in the winters, after his father and brothers had left Prouts Neck, he often visited them, going in particular to Boston every four or five weeks to see his father and make sure that the old man was in good health and eating properly.

Such a family relationship gives a bachelor the pleasures of domesticity without the restraints; however, since his closest associates remain those who shared his formative years, he is turned psychologically inward. In Homer's case there were additional pressures which drove him toward personal isolation.

A business career brings a man out into the world, but an artist is urged into solitude. He mines his own spirit. This delicate operation can be disrupted by exhaustion after a late social night, or shattered by interruptions. Whereas aging businessmen suffer from the danger of losing contact with themselves, aging artists are in danger of becoming hermits and losing contact with the world.

The summer people of Prouts Neck, on whom Homer's financial prosperity was based, were to him, as a painter, a confounded nuisance. He still needed, in the old Hudson River School manner, to walk about in search of the specific natural phenomena which would crystallize his emotions and enable him to paint. For the great seascapes he created at Prouts Neck he did not have to walk very far; the ocean beat against a cliff only a few rods from his studio door. But as Homer strode the rocks and dunes of Prouts, "hunting the best surf," he would frequently be interrupted by summer people out for a stroll and eager to call themselves to the attention of the celebrated artist. This was not only irritating for Homer; it destroyed his ability to paint. As he wrote to a friend from Civil War days, "Every condition must be favorable or I do not work and will not."

Worst of all were the amateur lady painters who wished Homer to pay deference to them as gently nurtured females while at the same time they talked to him as fellow artists. One of these, having rowed some distance across the bay with her father to call on Homer, was so outraged when he would not drop everything to receive her that she published a coy and spiteful account of his "rudeness" in the *Corcoran Art Journal*. This article, as much as anything else, helped fix on Homer a reputation as a bad-tempered recluse. In fact, he hated to be rude, but at the same time he had to protect himself and his ability to work. He had no gift for social chitchat, and while painting he was so intensely absorbed that he could not bear even a five-minute interruption.

To those who respected his privacy, however, Homer was a man of the greatest courtesy. He particularly enjoyed presenting ladies with bouquets of the flowers he grew in a small, carefully cultivated garden that adjoined his studio but was hidden from the world by a high wooden fence. Such bouquets also served as apologies when Homer had been gruff with someone but could not bring himself to say he was sorry.

On the infrequent occasions when the artist felt it necessary to mingle with his peers, he proved strangely sensitive to the impression he was making. He never went about unwashed like Ryder, nor did he, like Eakins, shock convention by appearing in incongruous cowboy or bicycling costumes. Instead, he dressed in the most meticulously conservative clothes which made him look, according to an observer, like "a successful stockbroker."

One of these public excursions took place in 1897. In that year, Homer's fellow artists gave him the greatest number of votes in an election determining the makeup of an art jury. The purpose of the jury was to select, from among the many pictures submitted, those that would be hung in the annual exhibition of the Carnegie Institute in Pittsburgh. Homer usually turned down such invitations, but this expression of the esteem of his colleagues so moved him that he accepted. However, to reassure himself he bought a brand new outfit of clothes, including necktie, hat and even cane. A lady painter, Cecilia Beaux, the fellow juror who had noticed the astonishing newness of Homer's costume, also noted that it "seemed to oppress the wearer a little." She was most surprised, however, to find that the painter of such energetic, forceful works was so small and slight. He revealed a high, bald forehead, a large hooked nose and a firm chin, but his mouth had disappeared behind a hedgelike moustache which was so dark that Miss Beaux wondered whether it had been dyed. With taciturn energy, Homer shared efficiently in the business of the occasion, expressing all the while an eagerness to get home.

But he was not completely retiring. At 11 o'clock on the first morning the jury met, Homer noted politely that when he was home he generally had an "11 o'clocker" at about that time. The jury adjourned

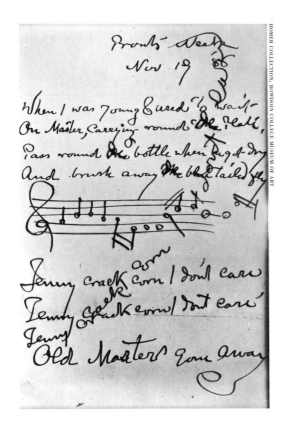

A man who liked his liquor—he spent about $40 a month on it—Homer had the common penchant for bursting into song when drinking. Here he has set down the words of "The Blue Tail Fly," in a meandering hand. Once when a friend asked what all the empty bottles were doing in his studio, Homer replied, "Don't know, John, I never bought an empty one in my life."

briefly to a bar that had been set up and then resumed its deliberations. At noon Homer made a similar modest suggestion, and so it went for the rest of the day and for the other days it took the jury to finish its work.

After his return home from Pittsburgh, Homer suffered from an attack of anxiety, imagining that someone had said something unfavorable about him. Such was his social insecurity that he felt impelled to write the director of the Carnegie Institute: "Something has appeared in the newspaper the nature of which I do not know. If it is in any way discreditable to me as I am led to suppose by certain remarks, *it is a great mistake.* . . . I wish to assure you that I am a man of truth and honor and worthy to associate with gentlemen." There is no evidence that Homer's fears had any basis in fact.

Homer was happiest at Prouts Neck, especially after the summer visitors had departed. The villagers did not impinge on him the way city people did. He would allow the local butcher to loll in his studio while he painted and even to criticize his work. He admired these people because, unlike the dilettantes from Boston and New York, they knew something practical and useful—how to hunt, or fish, or build a boat or shingle a house. He trusted their judgment. Homer kept quiet track of his simple neighbors, helping those who were down on their luck with gifts of cash which, in time, must have amounted to a considerable sum. He even managed to give one a needed wooden leg.

But for the most part, Homer remained alone. He seems to have liked it that way. In letters to his family and friends he insisted almost aggressively that he was happy and preferred the life he led to all others. Writing to put off a fellow artist who wanted to visit him, Homer succinctly described his isolated existence, and added some crusty reflections on its virtues. "I do my own work. No other man or woman within half a mile & four miles from railroad & P.O. This is the only life in which I am permitted to mind my own business. I suppose I am today the only man in New England who can do it. I am perfectly happy & contented. Happy New Year."

Often Homer was snowed in for days, the temperature remaining below zero. How did he pass his time when not painting? His neighbors were distant and he was not a reader. However, he enjoyed his own cooking, which he often did in his studio's big fireplace, and loved delicacies, ordered from a fine grocer in Boston. He also imported rum and whisky. In March 1903 he wrote his dealers: "The trouble was that I thought for a change I would give up drinking, and it was a great mistake, and, although I reduced the size of my nose and improved my beauty, my stomach suffered." He had four guns and two slingshots and a collection of coins. And he was an avid observer of nature. As he wrote his brother, "The Sun will not rise, or set, without my notice, and thanks." At times he could be most amusing about his solitary life, sending comic post cards and letters to his family, many of them illustrated. One of these shows three lobsters, evidently seeking shelter, heading from the shore toward the door of Homer's abandoned "portable painting house."

Where Ryder welcomed the role of hermit, regarding it as the true

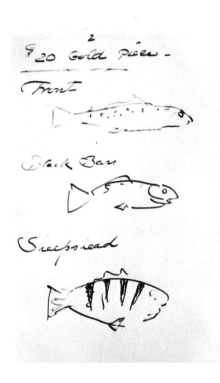

Homer's excitement over the new kinds of fish he was catching on a Florida vacation in 1904 led him to describe them to his brother Arthur. But, instead of using words, he resorted to pictures, noting only that the channel bass, which he soon made the subject of one of his watercolors, looked "like a new $20 gold piece."

artistic condition, Homer refused to accept this view of himself. He would indignantly deny that he could be described as "a recluse" or "an unsociable hog." He would expostulate: "I am working with a gang of men on a road I am building—I shall blast tomorrow. In fact I have little time to attend to my painting." But the undeniable fact remains that he was seeing less and less of the great world into which he sent his pictures. And in his self-imposed isolation, he often felt lonely, pushed to one side, undervalued.

The truth was exactly the opposite: during the 1890s Homer came to be considered in many important circles as the leading living American painter. Gold medals appeared in his Prouts Neck studio. He was, in his quiet way, proud of them. Once, spreading out a tightly rolled etching for a visitor to see, Homer silently put a gold medal on each corner to keep the paper from curling. Yet, in his darker moods, he insisted that he did not get enough encouragement to make it worth his while to continue to paint. In a confusion not uncommon with elderly artists, he seems to have felt that because he had withdrawn from the world, the world had withdrawn from him. Moreover, he was not experiencing the kind of success he had dreamed of as a young man. It enraged him that professional critics should write about his work, even favorably—why didn't they mind their own business? He did not wish the admiration of any specialized group. He still wished to feel at one with the wide American public that had taken him to its heart when he had been an illustrator for *Harper's*.

Of course, it was an impossible dream. Homer had moved away from the smiling view of life that had made him popular. In his art he had gone beyond the day-by-day American world. But still he complained of the obtuseness of the public, asking himself in moments of depression, "What's the use? The people are too stupid. They do not understand."

Homer's complaints were usually set off when some specific favorite among his pictures remained unsold. He would interpret this as a refusal of society to support him, and use it as an excuse when he hit a fallow period and could not paint. He had retired from "business," he would announce, adding dramatically, "I will paint for money any time." But whether or not the money came in, he would, as soon as creativity returned, go back to his easel.

Homer was never to achieve that smoothness of output which comes to middle-aged artists with established styles. His style never became fixed. In his acknowledgment of a $5,000 prize awarded him by the Carnegie Institute in 1896, when he was 60, he wrote: "Let us hope that it is not too late in my case to be of value to American Art in something that I may yet possibly do from this encouragement." Better than anyone, Homer knew that he was still learning, still experimenting, still growing.

During these crowning years of his career, Homer found subject matter primarily in four geographic regions: the Adirondacks, the Canadian North Woods, the Caribbean and, of course, Prouts Neck. In the Adirondacks, where Homer made many fishing trips with his brother Charles, the small watercourses and little lakes on which he angled and sketched were mere creases or dents in purplish evergreen forests. Since everything was lit from above and all colors were disclosed against dark foliage, Homer was carried back toward those contrasts of glowing and somber colors with which, 20 years before, he had first achieved the effect of brightness. In those naïve years, when he had silhouetted his gaudy croquet-playing girls against a cool background, the result had resembled a bugle call ringing out on a quiet day. But now Homer achieved effects more like a symphony, where the resonance of the bass reinforces the cry of the treble. Brightness became brighter. The wildest extremes were now in complete harmony.

In some of his more ambitious Adirondack paintings Homer managed color schemes so convincing, so right and, at the same time, so novel, that when the viewer's mind finally nudges aside his delighted eyes and he tries to analyze what the painter has done, he is hard put to understand how verisimilitude was achieved. In his *Adirondack Guide*, for example, Homer shows a forest pool whose gleaming water is shot with orange—and alongside it, dead branches that are a ghostly light blue. The trunk of a huge tree is also blue, though of a deeper shade. Sometimes he painted little canvases, like his close-ups of fish leaping from ebony and white water, which sparkle with such radiant color that they seem to belong less in an art gallery than in a jeweler's glittering display window.

In 1893 Winslow and his brother found more remote fishing grounds in the Canadian wilds north of Quebec. They built a cabin on the shores of Lake Tourilli from which, with professional guides, they set out on long wilderness adventures. The forest here was as unedited by the hand of man as was the ocean off Prouts Neck. Since the most volatile spirit was rushing mountain water, Homer often chose to paint the dramatic moment when frontiersmen brave the rapids in fragile canoes that cannot be stopped until the danger is past. Here he was less concerned with color than with movement, force, energy, balance. In the lightest and quickest of all artistic media, in pure watercolor from which virtually all line has been suppressed, Homer captured a vivid sense of the pull of the water, the buoyancy and the weight of the loaded canoes, the drag of the paddles—and also the solidity of rocks and the immobility of the background. All were joined into an inevitable and eternal esthetic whole.

The subject matter of many of Homer's Adirondack and Canadian watercolors is the savagery of nature and the echoing savagery of man. Savagery, of course, surrounds every human being every day. It is inherent in the meat that comes delicately cooked to the table, and it is inherent in all of mankind's conflicts—not only in fighting and war, but in selling and earning, in gaining love or fame or power. And the end of every man's life is savage: death makes no concessions to the politer virtues. Primitive peoples try in their art to make their peace with the savage aspects of life, but civilization usually turns its back, hoping that the blow will not fall today, or tomorrow. Homer did not turn his back.

After the horror, bloodshed and tragedy of the Civil War, the younger painters of the Hudson River School had by and large forsaken the wilder, more violent aspects of nature. They came down into the soft summer fields, staying, as one critic put it, "on the sunny side of the hedge." Homer, too, spent many years on the sunny side of the hedge, painting pretty girls, children, summer resorts. But, as his view of life became more profound, he turned away from the Hudson River School's identification of man with a benign nature. Instead, in his sea epics he painted man struggling for survival with alien and dangerous natural forces. Then in his wilderness scenes Homer swung back toward the Hudson River School attitude, again seeing man and nature as one. However, there remained a gap between his philosophy and that of his predecessors. They had identified man with nature's sublimity; Homer identified him with nature's savagery. His powerful pictures show humanity sharing with everything else alive the same inborn, desperate and at last hopeless struggle for existence.

Homer did not view nature as actively hostile; rather it was impersonal, neither friendly nor malign, neither good nor evil. This was a far cry from the Hudson River School's pantheism, which saw Nature as a manifestation of the goodness of God. Yet Homer adhered, with a stupendous underlying optimism, to the Native School's admiration for things as they are. He never mourned that humanity was embattled and savage. He found beauty in fierce strength, pride in the tough resilience of all animals, man included.

Man as a tough animal bent on survival is epitomized in Homer's fine Adirondack watercolor called *Guide Carrying Deer (page 124)*. In it a young woodsman carries the body of a deer he has killed across a wide, lumbered-over landscape. It is a somber fall day and he is sad, with the grave melancholy of the human condition. Around him the reds of autumn glow.

Concerning another painting, *Hound and Hunter*, the painter-critic Samuel Isham wrote that although the hunting of deer had been depicted for centuries, no artist but Homer would have shown a young guide sprawled on his stomach over the edge of a rowboat holding a half-drowned buck with one hand while trying to cut the animal's throat with the other. The scene, Isham pointed out, is hardly sportsmanlike. But Homer seems to have taken this for granted. When complimented on the picture, his comment—longer than most recorded about his works—ignored all moral and sporting implications: "I am glad you like the picture: it's a good picture. Did you notice the boy's hands—all sunburnt; the wrists somewhat sunburnt but not as brown as the hands; and the bit of forearm where the sleeve is pulled back not sunburnt at all. That was hard to paint. I spent more than a week painting those hands."

During the winter of 1898-1899, when he was 62, Homer renewed his earlier experience in the tropics, and several more seasons also found him in Nassau or Bermuda or Florida. As before, these sunny regions were for Homer both an actual world and a realm of fantasy. If in this wonderland he attempted sober themes, the tragedy was always muted. The Negro lying beside his shattered boat in *After the*

Tornado might as well be asleep as dead. In most of Homer's tropical watercolors, his youthful gaiety came back to him in full force and he now achieved his highest, brightest coloring. He did not, however, depend for brilliance on the elimination of dark hues, but traveled the whole gamut from black to the greatest brilliance, often in a single bold painting.

Homer's tropical experiences rarely found their way into the oils he painted after his return to Prouts Neck and, when they did, the results were various. His *Searchlight, Harbor Entrance, Santiago de Cuba* is supposed to comment on the Spanish American War, the searchlight standing for the American fleet that destroyed a Spanish fleet in these waters. But the picture communicates only idyllic moonlight gleaming on an old fort. However, in *Gulf Stream (detail, pages 172-173)* Homer did face up to the fact that tragedy could strike even in his tropical Eden. The result is perhaps the most disturbing picture he ever painted. In it a Negro fisherman lies dazed on the deck of a small boat which has lost its mast. A waterspout approaches, and sharks swim around waiting for the Negro's helpless though still-living body to be thrown to them in the turbulent water.

At Prouts Neck, Homer did his own washing and cleaning. He put a board under his mattress to make it hard and complained about the soft hotel beds he had to sleep in when he went to Boston to visit. When he walked his beloved cliffs he hacked angrily with his cane at the elderberry bushes because they were too weak and floppy for his taste. He scorned the ocean when it was calm—"that damned pond," he called it then—but loved it in its angriest moods. An artist friend, John W. Beatty, and one of the few visitors Homer ever allowed to stay in the studio, described his passion for storms. "Homer hurried into my room, robed from head to foot in rubber, and carrying in his arms a storm-coat and a pair of sailor's boots. 'Come!' he said, 'quickly! It is perfectly grand!' For an hour we clambered over rocks, holding fast to the wiry shrubs which grew from every crevice, while the spray dashed far overhead. This placid, reserved, self-contained little man was in a fever of excitement."

During the mid-1890s, Homer continued to depict the relationship between human nature and untamed water. In one of the masterpieces of this era, *The Lookout—"All's Well" (page 90)*, he seems to sum up all the mystery of seafaring in a few simple but powerful symbols. A bell, copper-colored against a bright night sky in which stars are embedded; some ropes stretched vertically; the summarily indicated rail of a ship with a little rough water beyond; and the cut-off figure of a sailor in oilskins—that is all the viewer sees. Yet the eye is convinced of the existence of a large ship, and, while the picture's canvas remains motionless on the wall, the viewer senses that the image is rocking. One feels around the boat the vastness of the ocean and the strangeness and wonder of man's triumphant if puny movement across this gray expanse.

This painting communicates the mystery of the sea as many of Ryder's best works do—but how differently! Ryder depicted visions

Homer's father in his last years refused to think of himself as being old. Here his son has caricatured him doing something he was very good at—giving other people orders. "Lewis," he says to his patient and always obliging manservant, "plant those English split-peas in hills." Crowning his head is a cap reading "Perpetual Youth."

that formed themselves in his own brain, while Homer was so concerned with having something tangible to paint from that he searched the Boston wharves for just the right kind of bell that he could pose in the moonlight. Where Ryder's ocean is that of a mystic dreamer, Homer's reminds us of that other Homer who in the *Odyssey* sang of the sea in ancient times. His concrete images evoke the thunder of the sea fully as powerfully as Ryder's more poetic visions.

An idiosyncrasy of Homer's father was his insistence on the benefits of cold baths —for other people. In a letter to his brother Charles, Homer gleefully commented on this with the caricature shown above, under a title torn from a newspaper advertisement for "A Rub Down."

As Winslow Homer neared his sixties, people for the most part disappeared from his Prouts Neck pictures. In this last phase his approach was that of a pure seascapist. Now he would attempt to catch, in the slower and more ponderous medium of oil paint, the same sorts of instantaneous impressions that he had long caught in his watercolors. This was, paradoxically enough, easiest to do in pictures showing nature at its most violent. A storm is a creature of sustained mood— and Homer knew at which spots for each direction of wind the waves beat highest. After contemplating the surf and sorting out in his mind its exact color and texture, he would return to his studio with the image fresh in his mind and quickly transmit as much of it to canvas as he could.

Much more difficult problems were presented by evanescent light effects. Concerning *West Point, Prouts Neck,* he wrote, "The picture is painted *fifteen minutes* after sunset—not one minute before—as up to that minute the clouds over the sun would have their edges lighted with a brilliant glow of color—but now (in this picture) the sun has got beyond their immediate range & *they are in shadow.* . . . You can see that it took many days of careful observation to get this, (with a high sea and tide just right)."

Having started another canvas, *Early Morning after a Storm at Sea,* he watched vainly for almost two years for the same effect to occur again. Then, "on the 24th of February, my birthday, I got the light and the sea that I wanted, but as it was very cold had to paint out of my window and I was a little too far away and although making a beautiful thing it is not good enough yet and I must have another painting from nature on it." When the picture was finally completed, he had worked on it four times at widely spaced intervals, each session limited to about two hours.

Homer's late seascapes seem completely natural: the viewer is convinced that this is the way the sea actually looked. And one is flooded by a warm esthetic happiness incited by the paintings' colors. These hues are often far from established preconceptions of the ocean. Thus, the spray on the breaking wave that runs across *Summer Squall (pages 176-177),* as well as the foreground surf, is a surprising light blue, made all the brighter by contrast with the dark glistening of the waves that have not broken.

But of course the naturalism and the color are inseparable from the shapes—their weight, their balance, their movement. The viewer feels the flow of tide and undertow, the power of water striking against rock, the resistance of the shore. These elements are never detailed or picayune. Homer's late pictures rarely hit more than three or four dominant notes. Indeed, for all their naturalism, these works have the qualities moderns so admire in abstract painting. A viewer who had never seen the ocean might mistake Homer's seascapes, with their fulfilling interrelationships of masses and movements and colors, for nonrepresentational action paintings and consider him, with the mid-20th Century American innovators, an abstract expressionist.

One feels in these last oils, which mark the culmination of Homer's career, that the artist has made peace with the world and himself. Storm and movement, the wild and untamed have eventuated in pure beauty: stress beats on stress until all is equilibrium. The wheel has come full circle. These are visions as lyrical as any of Homer's youthful depictions of charming milkmaids, but now the lyricism does not glance off objects with a lighthearted joy but is inherent in the very order of things: the tides flow and the waves roar and somehow the spirit of man is satisfied.

As Homer painted these serene and balanced works, he became as a man more and more querulous. For three years he virtually gave up painting except for the reworking of an early oil. Then in 1908 he had a slight stroke. He still lived alone, but the local postman was instructed to knock on his door every day and, if the recluse did not shout a reply, to break down the door and do what was necessary.

In 1909, when he was 73, Homer had a last burst of creative energy. His *Driftwood (pages 182-183)* is one of his great oils. Then, in 1910, nature struck him blind. His family prepared to move him from his studio to his brother Arthur's cottage, but he said from his darkness, "I will stay in my own house." On September 29, 1910, he sat up in bed and announced that he was looking forward to "a smoke and a drink." Then he died.

During his final illness, so it is said, Homer kept in a pocket, where he could feel it, the gold medal he had been awarded by the Paris International Universal Exposition of 1890. It was not a gold medal of the first class such as flashier painters had won, but Homer seems to have cherished it as a proof that he belonged not only to the United States but to the world.

Now it is being increasingly realized that Homer does indeed belong to the world. This recognition has come slowly because the attitudes that impeded the growth of Homer's reputation in his own lifetime long persisted. Americans concerned with art remained so busy looking abroad that they were unable to see anything that rose spontaneously and originally at home—and in the competitive lists of international artistic fame, if a painter's compatriots fail to champion him, no one else will.

Yet, since Homer's work never sank into obscurity, his pictures have continued to present their silent testimony. And today the balance that was thrown so violently to one side by the Civil War and the Gilded Age is being righted: Americans are recovering from their depressed and provincial fright of their native culture. In the international pantheon, Homer is finding his rightful place as one of the truly great painters of the modern world.

Living with the Sea

The older he became, the more Homer talked about abandoning painting—"retiring from business," as he used to say—but he could not, even when he despaired of the public ever really wanting his "goods." During his years at Prouts Neck, he kept his eye on the ocean, watching it, observing its moods, studying its colors in summer squalls and winter storms. "You must wait," he once said about the weather, "and wait patiently until the exceptional, the wonderful effect or aspect comes." Each new piece of information, each new thing learned, enabled him to make the sea seem more real, more alive in his paintings. In accepting the challenge that lay just outside his studio door, he was able to show a steady development as a painter both in power and technique—to go on growing as an artist right up to the end of his long life.

Homer sought always to please himself first in his work. He was never tempted to rush a painting (although he could paint quickly), or to mass-produce or in any way cheapen his art. If at times Homer seemed frustrated, it was, in part, because fame took so long in reaching him. Yet when it arrived, almost too late for him to care, it did not change him. He continued to spend his winters alone at the Neck, "out of gun shot of any soul and surrounded by snow drifts," and he was just the slightest bit amused. "Only think," he wrote to a friend, "of my being *alive* with a reputation."

Family circle, taken in 1895 at Prouts Neck, shows Homer with his beloved fox terrier Sam, his favorite sister-in-law Mattie, and his 86-year-old father, who sits, massive and indestructible, on the very edge of the chair.

Pictures on pages 167-172:

Life for Homer at Prouts Neck was by no means all art. In his father's and brothers' absence, he acted as a real estate agent, watching after their extensive properties and the family's big house—shown above, with Homer's studio at the far left. His year-round tasks ranged from burning brush to building fences and, on one occasion, a wall, in front of which he is posing (below). But the heaviest responsibility that fell to him was the care of his father—"Old Father Homer," as the Prouts Neck residents used to call him. Homer recognized him as an eccentric and loved him for it manfully putting up with an outrageous personality that grew crustier with age. The father's quirks often became the butt of the son's teasing pen. Homer Sr.'s long hair, for example, prompted the artist to caricature him as a Prize Old Man, the superior even of the Circassian sideshow girl with her wild coif (above, right). Homer sent wry reports to his brother Charlie (right) about their incorrigible parent. Once he wrote, "Father is having a good time by not agreeing to mind his own business and retire." Another time: "Father hustling about trying to get himself in debt by fall."

But the care of his father was ever more of a burden, eventually keeping Homer from traveling and even

painting. Not until 1898, twelve years before his own death, was he relieved of this duty. True to form, the father died in an argumentative mood. He wanted communion, but when he learned from the clergyman who arrived to give it to him that the Episcopal Church expected confirmation to precede the sacrament, he rebelled. The minister was willing to yield, but the dying man now insisted that he would take communion only if the clergyman admitted that confirmation was completely unnecessary. This the minister could not bring himself to do, and so the Prize Old Man left life the way he had lived it—as a maverick.

Devoted brothers and passionate fishermen, Winslow and Charlie pose with their catch. Homer—wearing sneakers—liked to fish from the rocks, Charlie from his yacht. The artist was a good cook and availed himself of the Neck's bounty, including such fish as flounder and tautog, lobsters and young dandelion greens. He once playfully chided Charlie for worrying about his excess weight: "You do not eat enough or drink enough."

Homer carefully guarded his privacy and his time in order to be able to concentrate more fully on his art and those things he enjoyed doing most, such as fishing and gardening. This does not mean, however, that he rejected friendships. Among the natives of the Neck he had many friends, and he especially enjoyed children, whom he occasionally allowed into his studio when he was not painting. In the photograph above he is shown sitting inside his garden enclosure with Frank Coolbroth, the appraiser of the Homer estate and a friend with whom he took many nature walks around the Neck. The knobby, twisted furniture on which they sit was, by Homer's intention, uncomfortable: no visitor would be tempted to stay too long, and the artist could get back to whatever business was at hand.

A zealous gardener, Homer raised everything from pinks to corn—and at one time even tobacco, in an unsuccessful attempt to provide himself with a ready supply of fresh cigars. It was his habit to put a bouquet of his flowers on his sister-in-law Mattie's desk each morning, and he often gave bouquets to his neighbors. Upon the marriage of one of them, a woman he had watched grow from childhood into maturity, he sent Lewis, the family retainer, around on her wedding day with a small bunch of forget-me-nots.

Homer at work was not a man to be disturbed by anyone. Even Lewis, with whom he had a warm and respectful relationship, could go no farther than the studio door to pick up the dirty dishes (above, right). But in the spells between work Homer could be as affable as any man and even enjoy a laugh at his own condition, as in the cartoons at right.

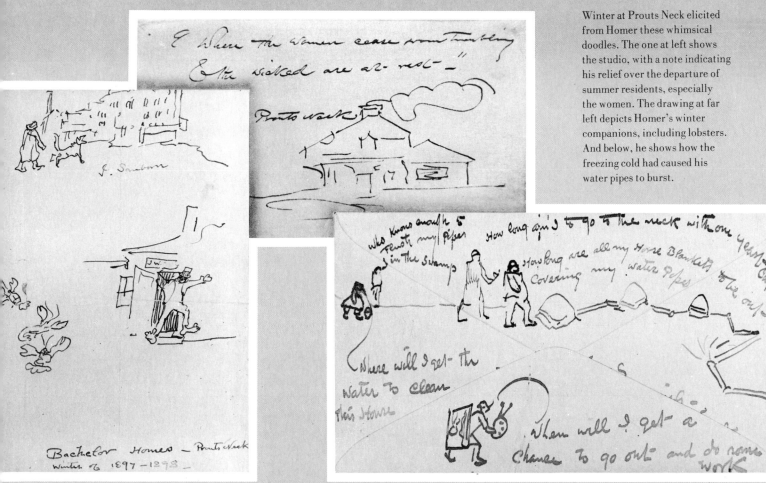

Winter at Prouts Neck elicited from Homer these whimsical doodles. The one at left shows the studio, with a note indicating his relief over the departure of summer residents, especially the women. The drawing at far left depicts Homer's winter companions, including lobsters. And below, he shows how the freezing cold had caused his water pipes to burst.

H̱omer is seen here bundled up against the cold in a unique photograph
—it is the only picture of the artist working in his studio. The painting on
the easel is, of course, his famous oil, *Gulf Stream*. Although it returns
to the perils-of-the-sea theme and the storytelling technique of his earlier
oils, it is nevertheless, as the detail opposite reveals, completely a product of
Homer's late style. There is a rich play of blues and greens in the water, and the
entire color scheme is intensified by the slash of red across the hull. But it is
in the powerful brushwork that the painting largely excels, the pigments
having been laid on the canvas thickly and rhythmically.

When *Gulf Stream* was first exhibited, some people found its subject brutal.
Homer, who generally kept himself aloof from his critics, became embroiled in
the controversy surrounding the painting. "The criticisms . . . by old women
and others are noted," he wrote his dealer sarcastically. "You may inform these
people that the Negro did not starve to death. He was not eaten by the sharks.
The waterspout did not hit him. And he was rescued by a passing ship."

Gulf Stream, detail, 1899

Among the many pictures Homer painted with a Prouts Neck setting, none is so hauntingly personal as this one— *Artist's Studio in an Afternoon Fog.* Carried out in shades of brown, it captures not only the quality of the mist that often veils the Maine coast in summer, but also conveys the enormous sense of isolation that Homer must have experienced when he lived here alone.

His studio is the building under the fog-dimmed sun. It was originally a stable. Made of wood, it faced squarely into the weather and had an open, second-story porch. The artist used to pace this porch for hours, observing the sea. He would often hang his paintings from its railing, then study them from the rocks, some 75 feet away, to check the effectiveness of his colors and composition.

The interior of the studio was spartan. The living room had a fireplace where Homer did his cooking, and a wooden bench, four straight chairs and a table. Next door was the painting room— "the factory," as he called it—built onto the studio as a gift by his brother Charlie. Upstairs, in the former hayloft, were his sleeping quarters, a room 22 by 17 feet furnished with a chair, a bed, a washstand, and a potbellied stove. During the winter months the studio was all but impossible to heat, yet he could write of long hours of dark, cold solitude, "I thank the Lord for this opportunity for reflection."

Artist's Studio in an Afternoon Fog, 1894

West Wind, 1891

Out of the long years he spent in Maine, Homer developed a deep understanding of the dynamics that made the weather and rocked the sea. His *West Wind (above)* captures the fury of gale-driven air and waves with a spontaneity suggesting how powerful the creative force could be in him. Painted quickly, it is one of those works that Homer used to say he finished by letting well enough alone—"which is the rule for grown artists only."

Summer Squall, with its surging waters and wind-tossed boat, would also seem to have been painted rapidly. But in fact it is the product of patient observation, followed by a dramatic episode and much hard work. The rock that is the focus of the composition Homer knew well: he had fished from it many times. But not until a squall blew up one afternoon did he get a chance to use it. Standing on the shore, he saw a sailboat being driven out to sea, loaded with children. Only the captain's sure knowledge of sailing saved them. Homer rushed off to set down his impressions; but when he began to paint the scene he did not include the imperiled children but concentrated instead on the sight of the sea erupting under the wind and churning through the crevices of the rock. Working steadily for two weeks, he brought the picture close to completion, then put it in a closet to wait for the inspiration that would allow him to add the final touches. The inspiration came in 1904—eight years later.

Summer Squall, 1904

Winter Coast, 1890

Fox Hunt, 1893

During the Maine winter, "shut out until I am dug out," Homer found
inspiration for two mighty oils—*Winter Coast* and *Fox Hunt*. In *Winter Coast*
a hunter with a Canada goose slung over his shoulder stands on the snowy
slope, watching the crashing surf. Homer took liberties with the locale, making
the slanting rocks more imposing than they actually are—thereby achieving
a far more forceful statement about man in nature than mere reality would
allow. *Fox Hunt* is Homer's largest canvas. It is not the fox that is doing the
hunting but the starving crows. They descend upon the animal as it plows
its way through the deep snow.

To paint this picture, Homer had neighbors bring him dead crows and
a fresh fox pelt. These he arranged outside his studio and allowed to freeze
in position. But the winter was already well advanced and, as he put it, "the
weather keeps thawing, and the crows get limp"—which may account for the
reaction of one of Homer's local critics, the stationmaster, who, upon being
shown the half-finished picture, remarked, "Hell, Win, them ain't crows."
Homer immediately painted them out, and replaced them with crows drawn
from life—lured within sketching distance by corn scattered on the ground.

A year before his death—and only a few months after recovering from a stroke—Homer tackled the theme of hunter and hunted once again in a painting even he considered surprising. Reproduced above, it betrays no sign of failing powers. Unlike the typical hunting scene, it is a vivid close-up of the hunter's target—two goldeneye

Right and Left, 1909

ducks shot as they rise from the choppy water. When a sportsman saw the still-untitled canvas, he let out a cry of recognition—"Right and left!"—the hunter's term for the feat of bringing down two birds with successive blasts of a double-barreled shotgun. The sportsman's exclamation became the title of the picture.

181

In the last year of his life, Homer seemed rushed. He had much to do. Even to his brother Arthur, he could only write, "*Cannot give you any more time.*" No one was to worry about him. "I am very well," he kept protesting, and he insisted that he was happy: "All is lovely outside my house and inside my house and myself."

But in truth he was not the same man he had been before his stroke, and he must have sensed death near, even though he let it be known that at 73 he was "making arrangements to live as long as my father and both my grandfathers—all of them over eighty-five." The digestive trouble that had plagued him in the past had returned. After an examination in New York, he announced, "It is only an acid stomach—all the other machines are in perfect order." But for only an acid stomach, it was giving him a great deal of discomfort. Stoical as ever, he saw no reason to complain, and he did not stop painting.

Driftwood (opposite) is Homer's last oil, and unlike many of his other seascapes of this period, it contains a figure. The small man, lost against the vastness of the sea, is trying to retrieve something from the water—a tree trunk the waves have washed ashore. A gusty, shifting wind drives the water from the left and right into a turbulent heap of foam. Nature seems to have gone out of control here, yet Homer, ill as he was, still had a firm grip on his brushes and his imagination. He knew, however, that this was his last picture. Adding the finishing touches, he smeared his palette and hung it on the wall. His lifetime's work was over.

Driftwood, 1909

Chronology: Painters of Winslow Homer's Era

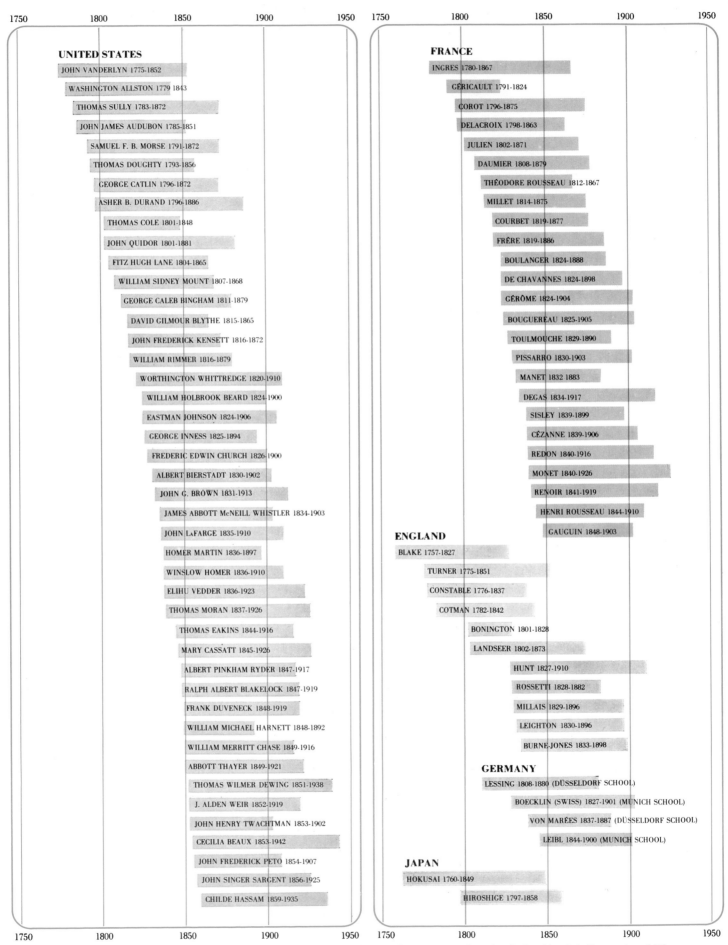

Homer's predecessors and contemporaries are grouped here in chronological order according to country. Lengths of colored bands indicate painters' life-spans.

Bibliography *Paperback

CULTURAL AND HISTORICAL BACKGROUND

Brooks, Van Wyck, *Dream of Arcadia*. E. P. Dutton & Company, 1958. The experiences of American literary and artistic travelers in Italy.

Carman, Harry J. and Harold C. Syrett, *History of the American People* (2 vols.). Alfred A. Knopf, Inc. 1952.

*DeVoto, Bernard, *Across the Wide Missouri*. Sentry Editions, 1964. Includes an account of some of the early painters of the West.

Mott, Frank Luther, *History of American Magazines*, Vol II, 1850-1865. Harvard University Press, 1957.

Davidson, Marshall, *Life in America*. Houghton Mifflin Co., 1951. A history illustrated with pictures authentically done at the time.

ART HISTORICAL BACKGROUND

Barker, Virgil, *American Painting*. Macmillan Co., 1950. A long, sensitive and personal essay.

Born, Wolfgang, *American Landscape Painting*. Yale University Press, 1948. A crotchety book, with valuable insights.

Clement, C. E. and Laurence Hutton, *Artists of the 19th Century and Their Works*. Houghton Mifflin Co., 1879. Two hundred and fifty brief biographical sketches.

Constable, William G., *Art Collecting in the United States of America*. Thomas Nelson & Sons, 1964.

Cummings, J.S., *Historic Annals of the National Academy of Design*. G. W. Childs, 1865. An invaluable archive.

Eliot, Alexander, *300 Years of American Painting*. Time Inc., 1957. Many color illustrations and a lively text.

Flexner, James Thomas, *A Short History of American Painting*. Houghton Mifflin Co., 1950. A quick, complete survey which has gone around the world, having been translated into more than 20 languages.

Flexner, James Thomas, *American Painting: The Light of Distant Skies, 1775-1830*. Harcourt, Brace and Co., 1954.

Flexner, James Thomas, *That Wilder Image: The Native School of American Painting*. Little, Brown and Co., 1962.

Hartmann, Sadakichi, *History of American Art* (2 vols.). L. C. Page & Co., 1901. A sympathetic book by a foreign observer.

Isham, Samuel, *History of American Painting*. Macmillan Co., 1927. Contains the best account of the "Younger Men."

Larkin, Oliver, *Art and Life in America*. Holt, Rinehart and Winston, Inc., 1960. A solid work, widely used as a textbook, that deals with all the fine arts.

Mather, Frank J., *Estimates in Art*. Henry Holt and Co., 1931. A scholarly critique of selected American artists.

*Museum of Fine Arts, Boston, *The Civil War: The Artist's Record*. 1961. Catalogue of a most informative exhibition.

Richardson, Edgar P., *Painting in America*. Thomas Y. Crowell Company, 1965. This often brilliant interpretation discusses more individual artists than any other survey.

Sheldon, G. W., *American Painters*. D. Appleton & Co., 1879. Accounts of artists then contemporary by one of the few men to interview Winslow Homer.

*Soby, James Thrall and Dorothy C. Miller, *Romantic Painting in America*. Museum of Modern Art, 1943. Expanded catalogue from a pioneering show.

*The Metropolitan Museum of Art, *Life in America*. 1939. Another pioneering show.

Tuckerman, Henry T., *Book of Artists*. G. P. Putnam's Sons, 1882. A many-faceted tome which contains more material on mid-19th Century American painting than any other single book.

Walker, John and Macgill James, *Great American Paintings from Smibert to Bellows*. Oxford University Press, 1943. A picture book, mostly in black and white.

WINSLOW HOMER, LIFE AND WORK

Aldrich, Thomas Bailey, "Among the Studies," *Our Young Folks*, July 1866. An interview with Homer during his early New York period.

Beam, Philip C., *Winslow Homer at Prout's Neck*. Little, Brown and Co., 1965. An intimate account of Homer's later years.

*Cowdrey, Mary Bartlett, *Winslow Homer, Illustrator*. Smith College Museum of Art, 1961. Contains a checklist of Homer's engravings.

Downes, William Howe, *Life and Works of Winslow Homer*. Houghton Mifflin Co., 1911. An early biography of Homer by a contemporary.

Gardner, Albert Ten Eyck, *Winslow Homer American Artist: His World and His Work*. Bramhall House, 1961. Includes an argument for a deep influence of Japanese watercolor on Homer's work. Nicely illustrated.

Goodrich, Lloyd, *American Watercolor and Winslow Homer*. Walker Art Center, 1945. An exhibition catalogue.

Goodrich, Lloyd, *Winslow Homer*. Macmillan Co., 1944. Long the standard biography of Homer.

*Goodrich, Lloyd, *Winslow Homer*, George Braziller, Inc., 1959. A shorter account by the author of the above.

James, Henry, "On Some Pictures Lately Exhibited," *Galaxy*, July 1875. An extended art review quoted in this volume.

Sheldon, G. W., "Sketches and Studies," *Art Journal*, April 1880. An interview with Winslow Homer.

OTHER ARTISTS OF THE TIMES

*Baur, John I. H., *John Quidor*. Munson-Williams-Proctor Institute, 1964-1965.

Benjamin, S.G.W., "A Painter of the Streets," *Magazine of Art*, 1882. A sketch of John C. Brown, the painter of newsboys.

Bryant, William Cullen, *A Funeral Oration Occasioned by the Death of Thomas Cole*. D. Appleton & Co., 1882.

Century Association, *Proceedings at a Meeting in Memory of John F. Kensett*, 1872.

Cowdrey, Mary Bartlett and H. W. Williams, *William Sidney Mount, 1807-1868, an American Painter*. Columbia University Press, 1944.

Durand, Asher B., "Letters on Landscape Painting," *Crayon*, 1855-1856. Durand's series of articles which set forth the principles of the Hudson River painters.

Durand, John, *The Life and Times of Asher B. Durand*. Charles Scribner's Sons, 1884. A standard biography by the artist's son.

Flagg, Jared, *Life and Letters of Washington Allston*. Charles Scribner's Sons, 1892.

*Flexner, James Thomas, *Thomas Eakins*. The Metropolitan Museum of Art, 1956.

*Goodrich, Lloyd, *Albert P. Ryder*. George Braziller Inc., 1959.

Goodrich, Lloyd, *Thomas Eakins, His Life and His Work*. Whitney Museum of American Art, 1933. The standard life.

Huntington, David C., *The Landscapes of Frederic Edwin Church*. George Braziller Inc., 1965.

Inness, George Jr., *Life, Art and Letters of George Inness*. Century Co., 1917.

Ireland, Leroy, *Works of George Inness*. University of Texas Press, 1965. Contains small reproductions of most Inness paintings.

Larkin, Oliver, *Samuel F. B. Morse and American Democratic Art*. Little, Brown and Co., 1954.

Mabee, Carleton, *The American Leonardo, A Life of Samuel F. B. Morse*. Alfred A. Knopf, 1943.

McDermott, John., *George Caleb Bingham, River Portraitist*. University of Oklahoma Press, 1959.

Miller, Dorothy C., *Life and Work of David G. Blythe*. University of Pittsburgh Press, 1950.

Noble, Louis Legrand, *Life and Works of Thomas Cole*. (E. S. Vesell, editor), Harvard University Press, 1964. A contemporary account recently reprinted.

Noble, Louis Legrand, *After Icebergs with a Painter*. D. Appleton & Co., 1861. An account of adventures with Frederic E. Church.

Pennell, E. R. and J., *Life of James McNeill Whistler*. J. B. Lippincott Co., 1911.

*Porter, Fairfield, *Thomas Eakins*. George Braziller Inc., 1959.

Richardson, Edgar P., *Washington Allston, A Study of the Romantic Artist in America*. University of Chicago Press, 1949.

*Rimmer, William, *Art Anatomy*, Dover 1966. Some 700 anatomical studies by Rimmer.

Ryder, Albert P., "Paragraphs from the Studio of a Recluse," *Broadway Magazine*, September 1905. Ryder's reflections on art.

Whittredge, Worthington, "Autobiography" (John I. H. Baur, editor), *Brooklyn Museum Journal*, 1942.

Whistler, James McNeill, *Gentle Art of Making Enemies*. G. P. Putnam's Sons, 1904.

Young, Dorothy, *Life and Letters of J. Alden Weir*. Yale University Press, 1960.

Picture Credits

The sources for the illustrations in this book appear below. Credits for pictures from left to right are separated by semicolons, from top to bottom by dashes.

Homer: *Eight Bells* (detail on slipcase). Courtesy Addison Gallery of American Art, Phillips Academy, Andover, Mass.

SLIPCASE:
Lee Boltin

END PAPERS:
Front: Frank Lerner
Back: Robert S. Crandall

CHAPTER 1: 6—Philip C. Beam. 9—From *Washington Allston* by Edgar P. Richardson, University of Chicago Press, 1948, plate II. 10—Yale University Art Gallery—from *The Telegraph in America* by James D. Reid, 1886, courtesy New York Public Library. 12—From *Harper's Weekly*, September 13, 1873. 14—Wadsworth Atheneum, Hartford. 17—Henry Beville. 18—Robert S. Crandall (2). 19—N. R. Farbman. 20, 21—Left: Frank Lerner (2); Robert S. Crandall. 22, 23—Robert S. Crandall. 24, 25—Henry Beville except top left: Metropolitan Museum of Art. 26, 27—Frank Lerner.
CHAPTER 2: 28—Lee Boltin. 30—Museum of Fine Arts, Boston. 32—Walter Daran. 34—From *Leslie's Weekly*, August 2, 1856, courtesy New York Public Library. 37—Al Asnis. 39—Donald E. Johnson. 40—LeBel's Studios

—Philip C. Beam. 41—A. Y. Owen—Philip C. Beam. 42—Al Asnis. 43—From *The Life and Works of Winslow Homer* by William Howe Downes, Houghton Mifflin Co., 1911, p. 8.—Library of Congress. 44, 45—From *Harper's Weekly*, August 27, 1859.
CHAPTER 3: 46—Suffolk Museum and Carriage House, Stony Brook, Long Island. 49—Percy Rainford. 50—The Bettmann Archive. 51—From *Scribner's Magazine*, September, 1906. 54—Albert Fenn. 56—Fernand Bourges. 57—Albert Fenn. 58, 59—A. Y. Owen. 60—New-York Historical Society—Albert Fenn. 61—Robert S. Crandall. 62—Munson-Williams-Proctor Institute. 63—Frank Lerner; Henry Beville—Robert S. Crandall. 64, 65—Robert S. Crandall.
CHAPTER 4: 66—Herbert Orth. 68—Princeton University Library. 69—Metropolitan Museum of Art. 70—Philip C. Beam. 71—Al Asnis. 72—From *Christmastide*, James R. Osgood & Co., Boston, 1878. 73—Culver Pictures. 76—From American Art-Union Bulletin III, 1849, courtesy New York Public Library. 78, 79—From *Harper's Weekly*, July 12, 1862. 80, 81—Frank Lerner; Museum of Fine Arts, Boston—Metropolitan Museum of Art; Al Asnis. 82—Robert S. Crandall. 83—Harry Baskerville—Albert Fenn. 84, 85—Frank Lerner; National Gallery of Art, Washington, D.C.; Frank Lerner. 86, 87—Frank Lerner; Metropolitan Museum of Art. 88, 89—Frank Lerner; Henry Beville; Robert S. Crandall—National Gallery of Art, Washington, D.C.
CHAPTER 5: 90—Robert S. Crandall. 92—From *Harper's Weekly*, January 21, 1882. 93—New-York Historical Society. 95—From *Centennial Exposition* by J. S. Ingram, 1876. 97—Bulloz. 98—Donald E. Johnson. 103—James Marchael. 104, 105—Left: Fogg Art Museum—Henry Beville. Right: Philip C. Beam—Frank Lerner. 106—Metropolitan Museum of Art. 107—Al Asnis—A. J. Wyatt. 108, 109—Robert S. Crandall; Art Institute of Chicago. 110, 111—Henry Beville. 112, 113—Lee Boltin.
CHAPTER 6: 114—Lee Boltin. 116—Philip C. Beam. 119—Philip C. Beam. 121—Philip C. Beam. 123—Frank Lerner. 124, 125—Robert S. Crandall except lower left: Frank Lerner. 126, 127—Frank Lerner. 128, 129—Robert S. Crandall; Fogg Art Museum; Frank Lerner. 130, 131—Fogg Art Museum; Robert S. Crandall. 132, 133—Frank Lerner; Robert S. Crandall.
CHAPTER 7: 134—Lee Boltin. 136—From *Art Anatomy* by William Rimmer, 1877, courtesy New York Public Library. 138—Lawrence A. Fleischman. 139—Sheldon Keck. 141—Metropolitan Museum of Art. 142—A. J. Wyatt. 145—A. J. Wyatt. 146, 147—Franklin Institute—A. Y. Owen; A. J. Wyatt. 148, 149—Top: Robert S. Crandall (2). Bottom: A. J. Wyatt (2). 150—Philadelphia Museum of Art; Albert Fenn—A. J. Wyatt—Lawrence A. Fleischman. 151—Robert S. Crandall. 152, 153—Henry Beville; Robert S. Crandall. 154, 155—Henry Beville.
CHAPTER 8: 156—Harry Baskerville. 158—Philip C. Beam. 160—Donald E. Johnson. 163, 164—Philip C. Beam. 167—Philip C. Beam. 168, 169—Philip C. Beam except top left: Donald E. Johnson. 170, 171, 172—Philip C. Beam. 173—Robert S. Crandall. 174, 175—Henry Beville. 176, 177—Lee Boltin; Frank Lerner. 178, 179—Lee Boltin. 180, 181—National Gallery of Art, Washington, D.C. 182, 183—Robert S. Crandall. 184—Chart by George V. Kelvin. 186—Lee Boltin.

Acknowledgments

The editors of this book are particularly indebted to Professor Philip C. Beam, Chairman of the Department of Fine Arts at Bowdoin College and author of *Winslow Homer at Prout's Neck*, whose advice and suggestions in the preparation of the picture essays were invaluable.

They also wish to thank: Philip Allen, Museum Engineer, Franklin Institute; Jane Barbee, Photoduplication Service, Library of Congress; James M. Carpenter and Mrs. Doris Gardner, Colby College Museum of Art; Charles Chetham, Director, Smith College Museum of Art; Mary Bartlett Cowdrey; Louisa Dresser, Curator of the Collections, Worcester Art Museum; Wilson DuPrey, Joseph T. Rankin and Elizabeth Roth, Print Room, New York Public Library; S. Lane Faison Jr., Director, Williams College Museum of Art; The Fogg Art Museum; Joseph T. Frazer Jr., Director, and Louise Wallman, Registrar, The Pennsylvania Academy of the Fine Arts; The Frick Art Reference Library; Henry Clifford Gardiner, Curator of Paintings, and Hobart Lyle Williams, Philadelphia Museum of Art; Albert Ten Eyck Gardner, Associate Curator of American Painting and Sculpture, and the staff, The Metropolitan Museum of Art; Lloyd Goodrich, Director, Whitney Museum of American Art; Bartlett H. Hayes Jr., Director, Addison Gallery of American Art; Mrs. Charles R. Henschel; Mrs. Charles L. Homer; Donelson F. Hoopes, Curator of Painting and Sculpture, The Brooklyn Museum; Edward L. Kallop Jr., Associate Curator, Department of Exhibitions, The Cooper Union Museum; Caroline K. Keck; Maria Seavey Larrabee; Edward Lipowicz, Director, Canajoharie Library and Art Gallery; Thomas N. Maytham, Curator, Department of Paintings, and Eleanor A. Sayre, Assistant Curator, Department of Prints and Drawings, Museum of Fine Arts, Boston; S. S. Pierce Co.; Mrs. George Putnam; Norman S. Rice, Curator, Albany Institute of History and Art; Caroline Rollins, Yale University Gallery of Art; Mrs. Maxwell Savage; Carolyn Scoon, Curator of Paintings, The New-York Historical Society; Mrs. M. W. Stratton, Sterling and Francine Clark Art Institute; Frank Anderson Trapp, Professor of Fine Arts, and Margaret C. Toole, Assistant Curator, Amherst College Museum of Fine Arts; Robert C. Vose Jr., Vose Galleries, Boston; John Walker, Director, National Gallery of Art, Washington, D.C.; John Washeba; Mrs. A. Osborne Willauer; Richard P. Wunder, Curator of Painting and Sculpture, The Smithsonian Institution.

Index

Numerals in italics indicate a picture of the subject mentioned. Unless otherwise identified, all listed art works are by Homer. Dimensions are given in inches; height precedes width.

Index (continued)

Index (continued)